Apology for Dancing

RAYNER HEPPENSTALL

APOLOGY FOR
DANCING

FABER AND FABER LTD
24 RUSSELL SQUARE LONDON

First published in June Mcmxxxvi
By Faber and Faber Limited
24 Russell Square London W.C.1
Printed in Great Britain
At the Bowering Press Plymouth
All Rights Reserved

To

Maude Lloyd
One Critic's Homage

Note

This book is addressed as much to those who think dancing needs no apology as to those who fancy it may merit none. For it is, I am convinced, your characteristic enthusiast who is the Dance's worst enemy. That, at any rate, is my apology for myself and for this book. Odd snippets of what follows have already appeared, in *The Adelphi*, *The Criterion*, *The Dancing Times*, *The New English Weekly*, *Theatre Arts Monthly* and the book, *Art and a Changing Civilisation*, which Eric Gill did for The Bodley Head: to the people responsible for which publications I acknowledge, here, my indebtedness. I wish, also, to thank Mme. Marie Rambert and Nicolas Legat, for teaching me, ultimately, the Meaning of Tradition; Col. W. de Basil, for back-stage privileges at Covent Garden; and all the dancers (and all the other teachers) who have given me practical demonstration of this and that choregraphic or technical detail. For my illustrations, I am indebted to five different people. The photograph of Raden Mas Jodjana comes from the Raden Mas himself. The Riabouchinska and Toumanova photographs and the picture of Lichine and the de Basil corps (in *Les Cent Baisers*) are part of the yield of an exceedingly hazardous photographic expedition with Howard Coster. The old print, from the magnificent collection at the

Note

Mercury, is the property of Mlle. Derra de Moroda. Nicolas Legat provided me with his own drawings. And the rest is the work of Malcolm Dunbar: a young amateur who looks as though he may become the first photographer to have covered, at all adequately, this amazingly rich photographic territory.

R.H.

Glan Ceirw,
May, 1936.

Contents

Illustrations

13

Illustrations

Plate 8. *Les Sylphides*. Toumanova and Paul Petroff. The non-balletomane may care to compare this with the *Jardin aux Lilas* (Plate 12). Mlle. Svetlova in that, Mlle. Toumanova in this, are extended in an arabesque, the posture above all others in which the classical danseuse reveals the perfection or imperfection of her line. *Malcolm Dunbar Photograph.*   *facing page* 206

Plate 9. *Le Tricorne*. Léonide Massine. *Malcolm Dunbar Photograph.*   *facing page* 208

Plate 10. Lichine and the de Basil Corps in *Les Cent Baisers*. (Nijinska). *Howard Coster Photograph.*   *facing page* 210

Plate 11. *The Descent of Hebe*. Hugh Laing and Elisabeth Schooling. The production of such cinematographic effects as this, on the tiny stage of the Mercury, is a triumph of collaboration between choregraphic and scenic artists. Nadia Benois's three ranks of rose-muslin clouds are pulled upward, coïncidentally with the falling movement of one dancer, the straining back of another, and an immediate black-out of the stage. The illusion which Mr. Tudor has attempted, with these very elementary means, is theatrically (not naturalistically) complete. Music by Ernst Bloch. *Malcolm Dunbar Photograph.*   *facing page* 220

Plate 12. *Jardin aux Lilas*. (Chausson—Hugh Stevenson—Tudor.) *Left to right:* Antony Tudor, Maude Lloyd, Hugh Laing, Tamara Svetlova, Elisabeth Schooling. *Malcolm Dunbar Photograph.*   *facing page* 224

Apology for Dancing

'So that gestures, not music, not odours, would be a universal language, the gift of tongues rendering visible not the lay sense but the first entelechy, the structural rhythm. . . .'

—ULYSSES

I. Intentions

In any broad thoroughfare, you are vaguely oppressed by the miscellaneous unloveliness of the human beings who throng there. You take to yourself their aimlessness or strained intentness, the heavy unsatisfaction shown in their faces and the wasteful effort and carelessness of their movements. And then somebody passes with conspicuous grace, with something near flawless economy and ease of proud movement, whether quick or slow, and a face that shows either eagerness or gentle contentment. And your mind seems translated, in the sudden answering pleasure, to another level of experience, altogether. Quite probably your pulses quicken, and your own gait becomes smoother and more handsome, or possibly only the muscles of your face relax, and you smile.

Either way, that answering pleasure is in the same kind as the pleasure to be got from Ballet. You say, of the proud-moving person, that he 'fairly dances along', and it is said literally, not as metaphor. Good walking embodies the conditions of good dancing. There is a human body moving according to some spontaneous realisation of its own harmonic laws, so that there is no waste of energies, but economy, only, and the greatest possible muscular efficiency.

And all this in obedience to a definite sustained rhythm.
. . . Organic rhythm, it is certain (heart's beat and the puls-
ing of blood through all the body), but the rhythms of
Music are related to organic rhythms and affect us powerfully only by their stress and interaction with these. That
proud mover shows in his face, too, the conditions of a
spiritual harmony. Eagerness or gentle contentment is,
shall we say, the spiritual correlate of the harmony of physical movement, its content. And, in your own nervous and
muscular response, the mind does shift to another level of
experience, which is experience in the æsthetic order.

This, then, is the main conception of Ballet that I want
to elaborate. Ballet, first of all, and with the Dance as a
whole, is human bodies behaving in an unusually lovely
manner, seeming to tend towards an ideal pattern, the Pla-
tonic Idea of movement. The condition of all such lovely
behaviour is perfect obedience to certain rhythmic and
harmonic laws, which are all plainly and baldly organic in
origin. And the æsthetic response is more nervous and muscular than merely visual and intellectual. Dancing, generally, is a great heightening of the natural tensions of human
movement. Ballet, in particular, is such a superlative
heightening, such a complete epitome and pure essence,
that it will often have to be regarded, in the contrary sense,
as an absolute and closed art, which must not be adulterated with lower forms of dancing. And Ballet in the Theatre involves a great deal more than the interplay of human
bodies, being, in its perfection, of almost unreckonably
complex structure. The first insistence must be, none the
less, that Ballet arises in common organic processes and is
so profoundly rooted there that it can be fully understood
only by reference to every other order of human activity.

Intentions

Not to some orders, only, but to every order, of human
activity. . . . Later on, I shall set Ballet, in opposition to
the Hindu Dance, against the whole religious and cultural
background of the West, and present it as not only an expression but also a partial explanation of the Western
spiritual and intellectual habit. And it is plain enough that
Ballet will constantly have to be related to the other forms
of Art, the other heightenings and focuses of natural behaviour: with such close relation that we can often expect
to hale out principles, working in Ballet, which will give
us new critical insight into Poetry, as well as into those
arts, of Music, Drama, Painting and Sculpture, whose connection with the Dance is more direct and obvious.

Ballet, in fact, can become a whole mode of consciousness, in terms of which there is nothing that cannot be
partly restated. To know Ballet is to know most other
things in one more way. You might talk of the Choregraphic Vision of Life, which William Blake had, for one,
in a baffled kind. But a perhaps more fundamental need, at
various points, will be to give Ballet its place in the contemporary scene. So much digression will be necessary,
more than once. For, certainly, Ballet as it is at present can
mean something definite only in relation to Society as it is at
present. No art can ever exist entirely in a vacuum (unless the private phantasy of the lunatic be accepted as art),
and Ballet—as a form of the Dance and, at the same time,
as a Theatre art, made in the fusion of four arts otherwise
self-sufficient—depends, as much as or more than any
other art-form, on communal response. The conditions of
the existence of Ballet, at any given historical moment, are
essential conditions of Society as a whole, in its actual historical phase, and the very much confused status of Ballet,

19

to-day, takes its meaning from the confused characteristics of what we call This Age or the World in Our Time.

Ballet, as it exists in to-day's theatres, is affected, along with the other arts and the other forms of the Theatre, by all the mad characteristics of the age. There are plenty of healthy Englishmen shocked to the soul by moonlight and muslin; or literary huskies, like Wyndham Lewis, who are goaded, by the evident and undoubted attraction of Ballet for the two or three kinds of markedly incomplete person, into combing out the hair on their chests and roaring large and blithely about 'Diaghilev's epicene circus'. And their instincts are not entirely stupid, though they are misdirected. Those whose blind spot is Ballet would, in fact, be even more outrageous in their antagonism if they knew the inwards of balletomaniac officialdom. Ballet Criticism, for one thing, always has been, except with Noverre and Fokine, a more contemptible craft than Literary Criticism or even than Music and Plastic Criticism, and, intellectually, a gathering of the pundits of Ballet is not clearly distinguishable from, say, the deliberations of a poultry-fanciers' association. Ballet, moreover, in this still bourgeois world, is often as purely commercial in intent as Shaftesbury Avenue and is still surrounded with something of the glamour of an Imperial-Court harem, so that both the more meretricious stage aspects and the off-stage personalities of dancers are still sadly overstressed.

These things, all the same, have not affected the Dance in its essentials. In later chapters, I shall be much concerned both with these more obvious and with subtler evils, which the believer in Ballet as a serious art must abominate more than anyone can whose interests are altogether apart. But all these are the environment, only, of

Ballet, and have not tainted down to its substantial self, as similar things have tainted down in the other arts. The organic central tradition persists, as it persists nowhere else, and the cause is very largely in that nervous and muscular rather than merely intellectual response which Ballet necessarily calls out. Ballet cannot become inwrenched, like all the other arts, now, without ceasing to be Ballet.

According to Walter Pater, the duty of Art, and of the several arts, is to aspire to the Condition of Music. And the Condition of Music is, perhaps, a form of Abstraction. So that Ballet will tend, will aspire towards the inwardness of the other arts? But it is as it were a revivified order of Abstraction, strongly rhythmed and operating directly, sensuously. Such equipoises of Passion as cancel out passions, yet do them no violence. . . . The making of not-final statements of experience: with the interlocking of these statements into experiential patterns that are final. . . . A neutralisation, an apparent Stasis, which is yet intensely vital and powerfully dynamic. . . . Something like that, in so far as the Condition of Music is capable of definition. . . . And the possible stress, here, the measure of excellence, the standard of value, is certainly not in Abstraction, not in the Condition itself, but in the force and range of contradictory human elements—passions, impulses and the rest—which are leashed and welded, balanced, cancelled and neutralised, in apparent subservience to a particular abstract form. An abstract, a general idea, the Condition of Music, is easy to attain; but is attained, every other where than in major works of art, by violation of the minute particulars, cooking of the experiential data. Excellence, in art, is measured—so—less by the perfect coherence and fusion of parts than by the range and strength of parts and their stubborn resistance to coherence and fusion, the difficulty with which, to bring them to the Condition of Music, the order of pure forms, they are reconciled. And it is on this principle, out of which, also, a way, a method, of feeling and loving Ballet can be got, that the excellence of Ballet, as a medium, proves itself.

For the primary art-material of Ballet is human bodies, and the human body, being the most complex and the most strongly individualised of all organic and inorganic things, resists fusion, resists cohesion with its own kind and with other kinds, more energetically than any other art-material can. Ballet is a continuing struggle—of mind against matter, you might say, but rather of general against particular. It derives from, and subsists in, tensions. With the dancer, it is a struggle between a wastefully complex muscular system, designed for a limited range of animal acts and offices, and the economy, the simplicity, in line and mass, of the postures and movements—the Physical Ideas—to which his body, as a material of art, aspires. With the choregrapher, it is a struggle between coherence and fluidity, between his desire for harmony, among bodies whose original sin is to desire each to be its own single harmony, and his desire for progression in continuity, the need to be destroying each harmony in the instant of its achievement, resolving it into another, and another, and another, so that no appearance of finality shall be possible until the interflow has worked itself out in a pattern which the mind can contemplate as significant and therefore as static.

And, with the spectator, it is a struggle between the rigid habit of his eye and the need to contemplate his perceptions musically, a struggle resolved through kinæsthetic response, through muscular sympathy, nervous empathy, inscape. Ballet must be felt by the spectator in that way. Ballet, viewed as a structure, a system of tensions, is human beings behaving in the Manner of Music. It is not a mixture of Music and Pictures and, if you like, Acrobatics, but a fusion of these. It is human bodies, themselves constituting pictures, designs in Space, their separate movements interacting like musical phrases, like the idiom of a language, in such a way that the designs in Space become designs in Time, also, projected into rather than accompanied by the actual music of the orchestra, which itself, thereby, becomes spatially significant. And this makes up, as a single whole, the organic structure of life itself, simplified into manageable forms and making possible an immediate directness of response.

So much, then, for the general significance of the structure of Ballet. . . . It may appear to be too much, as the preliminary statement for what, first of all, is simply a pleasure, a particularly keen and subtle kind, at its best, of delight. But it is nothing, after all, to what is claimed for Poetry and Music, as revelations of the Absolute, or in the statement of Dr. I. A. Richards and his followers, who are many, that Poetry Alone is Capable of Saving Us. This, however, covers only the general order, the Dance. I have yet to justify my treatment of Ballet as the Dance's supreme form.

'Ballet . . . is such a superlative heightening, such a complete epitome and pure essence'—which is to say, of the natural tensions of human movement—'that it will often have to be regarded, in the contrary sense, as an absolute and closed art, which must not be adulterated with lower forms of dancing.' But is it so? Many who ac-

cept my general statement on the Dance and who may
have been pleased by my opening paragraphs, though they
sounded rather like an advertisement for the Schools of
Deportment, will find it difficult to agree that Ballet is so
definitely the highest form of the Dance. They will say
that Ballet is an art of spectacular tricks and whimsies, a
tradition of silly flutterings and nonsensical mimic gestures, which will not let it free itself of the gauzy tip-toed
sylphs, birds, flowers and animated dolls, its only manageable themes. And Ballet is so exclusively a feminine art that
its male dancers, shaven, painted and generally ætherial-
ised, cannot be anything but ridiculous or nauseating.

In fact, Ballet is unspeakably artificial, epicene and altogether devoid of seriousness, and all the significance it
may lately have acquired is due to its incorporation of the
more emancipated dance-forms—to a wise desertion of
its post as 'an absolute and closed art', etc. And this is a
case so often and so plausibly made out, both by literary
gentlemen and by those who wish to express their own
peculiar personalities in the Dance, that it cannot be re-
futed all in a moment. It is a case, I think, which depends,
most often, on a morbid insensibility, for it is very much
like the tone-deaf Charles Lamb's case against Music. But
quite intelligent people support it. My friend, Michael
Sayers, for one . . .

*'I was so far reduced that if a troupe of youths and maidens had
come out dancing a ballet on the stage I might have sat up and
smiled, though in less anæsthetised mental states nothing seems
to me less endurable . . . than the marionettish antics and acrobatics of balletic prancers.'*

And Mr. Sayers is not only among our best young critics
of the Drama. He is also a notable supporter of several

kinds of Free Dancing, with which I shall later have to deal.

My own present view is best stated, perhaps, by saying that an Apology for Dancing necessarily means, for me, a Book about Ballet. 'All dancing is urgent and substantial life'—and so on, and, in so much, it is good. But so is an elephant. So is a plague of green fly. So is an aspidistra. Other qualities are needed, for urgent and substantial life in art. I have already hinted, for instance, at precision, speed and beautiful line, in continuity of style. And I see all other forms of dancing—all European forms, at least— as merely preparatory to Ballet, in their embodiment of such qualities: as Prose, in its various forms, may be considered a field in which situations are argued out, refined and at last fitted for statement in Poetry. Ballet, in this view, and Ballet in its very purest sense, is to the Dance as a whole what European Poetry is to Literature as a whole. More succinctly—mathematically—

Ballet : Dancing : : European Poetry : Literature.

And it is a view which I want, in this book, to justify to the full and communicate, to the literary-minded and to 'healthy Englishmen', as well as to the uncertain because temperamental and often pathological addict and to the general view, even, of thoroughly intelligent followers of the Ballet, who, for the most part, are really less interested in the Ballet itself—that is, in the dancing—than in adventitious literary content, musical basis, or, more intelligently, in the purely visual, plastic, pictorial value of the spectacle. But it is a view which takes some reaching, if one's education is not of Bloomsbury, nor yet of the even more bogus Hampstead.

This book will undoubtedly be called provincial, altogether (as well as reactionary). And so it is. Its standard is the Provinces. That is to say, it dislikes the hot-house Metropolitan. It looks to Everyman—though, certainly, to an ideal Everyman—as the last judge, or the last but one, and not to the febrile values of the Timekept City. But the only point, here, is that my own first experience of Ballet was in the Provinces, and I was a very provincial youth, indeed, when I underwent it. Stanislas Idzikowsky danced, and I cannot remember who else, in *Les Sylphides* and *Le Spectre de la Rose,* and I cannot remember what else, one Saturday afternoon, when I should have been playing cricket. I had lately become very culture-conscious, especially in a musical way, but I was still at school, afflicted with the aggressive heterosexuality of one just growing away from our homosexual English pedagogic values, and what I characterised as 'these bloody muscular nancy-boys' offended me very much. I had learnt beforehand—from some weekly culture-journal, I suppose—that Ballet was a subtle and sublime form of Art, with a very big capital letter. And all I saw was fluttering sylphs in muslin (though they had the most admirable legs) and men who combined a fearful muscular development with what seemed to me an obvious, a flaunted and unnecessary effeminacy of movement—and all this to the music of Chopin and Weber, which I had already been taught to spurn.

My reactions were, I fancy, typical of the Provinces and Provincial London, as a whole, and therefore significant, which is the only reason why I make this passage autobiographical. At any rate, I was not induced to visit the Ballet again for several years, and, when I did (in London now), it was not Classical Dancing which again and again kept me going, but the modern ballets and pseudo-ballets, with their 'simplification of current life into something rich and strange'. Sylphs, swans and animated dolls I still found rather sickly and preferred the more exotic glamours, grotesqueries and slick satire of the Diaghilev ballets.

That long phase—apparently the phase of appreciation at which the balletomaniac normally stays put—was finally and violently terminated by Massine's *Union Pacific*. This ballet was a great revelation. I had never, in my life, seen anything quite so irritating and futile in a grand way, or any single work that embodied so much of the Bigger and Better, the Louder and Funnier, and I was goaded by it into producing my first piece of Ballet Criticism. *Union Pacific* was, in fact, or seemed to me to be, a reduction to the absurd of the whole trend of Ballet since Fokine left the Diaghilev Company, and I, for one, felt utterly bewildered and betrayed. The consequence was that I went and sat at the feet of Nicolas Legat, in Fulham, and would have nothing, for a long time, but the purest of Pure Classicism and Technique for Technique's Sake.

Et cetera. . . . The moral of this telescoped history is that you have to be taken in and disgusted, taken in again and worried out of your life, before Ballet 'begins to dawn on you'. Ballet is altogether a theatrical art, but you have to grow heartily sick of the Theatre, and desert it for the Classroom, before the significance of the Theatre becomes apparent. Ballet as Pure Muscular Style, in whatever conventional setting, is the most significant Ballet, and, so far as I can see, before the axiom is proved upon your pulses, you have to sit, for hours, learning to feel its forms along your own nerves, watching dancers and will-be dancers, in the quite glamourless practice dress, of black tights and any other odd thing, doing pliés and battements and ronds des jambes par terre, at the very prosaic bar. The Critic, the serious onlooker, in fact, needs a training, not so strenuous, nor so lengthy, but quite as concentrated as that of the Dancer.

In the course of which he becomes newly conscious of the process that History is. . . . That Muscular Style, which Ballet most fundamentally is, must be seen as the product, but not the end-product, of centuries of the Dancer's struggles against the natural stupidity of his body. With all its concomitant artificialities, it is an amazing achievement in itself, fruitful for much contemplation without any regard to the great range of its applications in the Theatre, though it belongs to, was evolved for, the Theatre. And this evolution is always intimately intertwined with significant changes and developments in the social status of the Dance and of the Theatre. The process of Ballet is an abstract of the evolutionary process of Society. It is in terms of such a belief, at any rate, that I wish, now, to lay out the more purely historical and geographical part of my argument.

II. Moonlight and Muslin

A. Some Beginnings

The Origins of Ballet are, as the serious works of History say, lost in obscurity, though David danced, we know, before the Ark, and the Greeks are believed to have run about, on lawns and urns, very much after the fashion of Miss Ruby Ginner. In fact, the direct lineage of Ballet refuses to be traced back beyond the Renaissance, and there was no sign of Ballet proper until the end of the seventeenth century. The Egyptians danced, six thousand years ago. Worried historians have even tried to convince themselves that those leaping figures, in their tombs, were executing entrechats. The Greeks danced, deriving from the Egyptians, and we have thousands of images of their dancing, from which Raymond Duncan, among others, constructed a system. Sometimes, even, the figures on the Grecian urns appear to be turned out, in the Ballet sense. In Rome, there was professionalism, as we know it to-day. But the concrete evidences we have, of the forms that preceded Ballet in the West, permit nothing more than a broad historical argument, which is bound to be more metaphysical, in any case, than merely honest.

Moonlight and Muslin

And History's most important showings, for these times, are all of Status, not Style. A rise and fall of Status, with changing forms, and a concentration on Form increasing as Status diminishes . . . I shall try, later, to show how dancing is all religious in origin, in what I believe to be a quite new sense, but in Ancient Greece certainly (in Ancient Egypt, supposedly) dancing was, more than anything else, a religious exercise, a ritual: as it is, to our own day, in most Eastern countries and in most barbarous and savage regions. Greek Tragedy, which is surely our best endowment from the Ancient World, began as ritual dancing and choral chanting. It was an expression of the religious wonder and terror of the whole community. Individuality was lost in it. There was utter impersonality, before a mystery. The mystery was ineffable. Only Gesture would not profane it, only the ecstatic movements of the dedicated human body. And then there was a splitting away. The ritual was intellectualised and individualised. A scientific curiosity asserted itself against an inchoate fear, in the face of the inscrutable and transcendental. The mind wished more to comprehend than to propitiate or to enter into any passional relation. Naturalism appeared, deliberate imitative art, and forms projected rather from the head than from the solar plexus, the centre of immediate passional response. Solo actors appeared: one, at first, and then more with Æschylus, more with Sophocles, more with Euripides. And Euripides, at last, had turned Tragedy towards the modern problem play.

Friedrich Nietzsche, just now, is in danger, because of the steel rods and castor oil used in his name, of becoming as unpopular, again, as he was in war-time. But he is our greatest historian. To him, this development of Greek

Some Beginnings

Tragedy was decadence, was the Fall of Man. It was the expression of the intellect's Will to Power, to dominate fear and the world of fear by abstraction and assert this control against the community, in self-distinction: either by self-isolation or by taking up the part of demagogue. It was a transition from ecstatic pagan living, with its joyousness and its terror, to the probing fidgety generalisations of 'the old bore, Socrates'. Evidently, this bears on my first chapter's argument, in so far as this transition is not complete until our own time, and it bears even more on what comes in later chapters. For the moment, we can use Nietzsche's terms and speak of a change from Dionysian to Apollonian dancing, from Passion to Style, from cosmic frenzy to a search for formal perfection. And the Greeks perished, when Apollo had not only overcome but also banished Dionysus.

From Athens to Rome, then. . . . The split becomes more distinct, there. The Dance becomes pure entertainment, and dancers a professional class. Apart from certain esoteric sects, who, occasionally, presented facets of their dancing mystery to the populace, for purification, there was no religious element in the Dance at all, towards the end of the Græco-Roman civilisation. And Religion, in its first sense, means simply that which binds a community together: all its ritual exercises, its expressions of solidarity. But, compared with the Greeks, the Romans were a dull people, altogether, an aggressive bullet-headed people, something between militaristic Prussia and commercial America. And nearly all their extant art is uninteresting. Their dancing, we may suppose, was energetic and efficiently presented and, in The Decline, a powerful aphrodisiac. But when, with The Fall, we come to a quite different civilisation, the Christian civilisation, with its new cultural energies (though dominated by a spiritual Rome), we find that the Dance holds, again, the status that it had in The Glory that was Greece.

For Church Ritual must be accounted the major medieval form of the Dance, the Christian equivalent of Greek Tragedy. It was slow, quiet, processional, heavily dressed, asserting Spirit against Flesh, and greatly contrasted, in its highly developed choregraphic forms (with liturgical response as their basis), to the leaping naked forms of the Dionysian orgy. But it was a communal function, a binding together of the community in shared ecstasy. And the Church controlled the popular forms of dancing, also, which grew and had grown up around her: not so much in the way of censorship as in the way of sanction. A holiday, a merry-making, was always a Church festival, a holy day, a spiritually legalised Saturnalia. Sacred and Profane were intimately linked together, and solidly, despite the occasional fulminations of some of the more fanatical ecclesiasts. To the time of the Renaissance, then, the European forms of the Dance, excepting one period of decadence, were, like the Eastern Dance, a communal religious function. Splits occurred, in the times of decay, but, dominantly, there was synthesis. And there was no separation of the Dance from the Drama, from Poetry and Painting, Architecture and Music. All the forms of art grew and flourished together, around the Church or the Temple. With the Renaissance, the far more complex modern process begins, in Society as a whole and in the Dance, as it develops, alongside the other arts, within Society's forms.

The Renaissance, most clearly, was two things. It was an assertion of Individuality, and, in its other guise, as the

Reformation, it was Secularisation. The two things fuse. Individualism in Religion is Secularism. In the basic sense of Religion, Protestantism is irreligious. Give a man the idea that Religion is a matter between God and himself, with the Church as little more than a clearing-house, and, in practice, he will tend to equate himself with God. Or else he will deny God. For the Individualism of the Renaissance was basically economic, and so was the Reformation. The seeming expansion of creative and spiritual vision simply reflected an actual expansion of fields of commercial endeavour and the means to exploit other men by the accumulation of economic power. The Brave New World was El Dorado, and the God who ruled it had said nothing about camels and the eye of a needle. Leonardo da Vinci is one symbol of the Renaissance. Hamlet, possibly, is another, though he might be better considered as an atavism, a religious survival in a lay world, one left over from the Middle Ages. Neither, in any case, is so characteristic of the Renaissance as the Usurer is. And the Borgias, Vittoria Accorambona, Francesco Cenci, were one other kind of quattrocento and cinquecento Economic Individualism, spreading itself into the field of Ethics, with Machiavelli as apologist, at a rather higher level of awareness than their own.

At any rate, the history of the modern world is a tale of increasing Individualism, increasing self-distinction and self-assertion, in all social, cultural, intellectual and spiritual fields: until, at the present day, when there is no more room for personal endeavour (except where some single colossus, like Diaghilev, Horatio Bottomley or Mme. Blavatsky, breaks through), Individualism either degenerates into eccentricity or is replaced by combines, syndicates, cartels, leagues, unions, sects and schools, forms of getting together which are as different from religious community as democracies are from Democracy. And, certainly, there is no great religious art in modern times: none, in Europe, since the Renaissance. If Religion is a matter between God and the individual soul, there must be no powerful outward showing to record and compel community of experience. There must be as little as possible to distract the individual soul from communion with itself. Men must still congregate, in the name of Religion, but the places of their congregation and their forms of religious exercise must be as bare and simple as dignity will allow, God's dignity or Man's. Consequently, elaborate Ritual is denounced as mere empty show. The great cathedrals become tourist spectacles, as little relevant to the common life as the Parthenon or the Colosseum. And all great communal poetry, music and devotional image-making disappear. Instead of religious art, there is devout art, which reached greatness only once, perhaps, in Johann Sebastian Bach. And in him, too, there is a great deal of virtuosity. His masses sound wrong, even faintly vulgar, as masses, beside the masses of Palestrina. Or there is the work of individual Dionysians, like William Blake and D. H. Lawrence, which is religious in the sense that it clamours, even howls, for a return to Religion, a revolution of the most desperate kind.

See the order, briefly, in which the various arts split themselves away from their first religious function. . . . As it had been with Greek Tragedy, solo actors began to appear in Church Ritual. There had always been the officiating priest, with his attendants, but he was rather the leader of the chorus than a solo actor. The forms of liturgical response, then, were intellectualised and individualised, extended into the first kinds of Medieval Drama. At one level, the great religious mysteries were celebrated in the perfect form of the Mass. At another, they had to be humanised and celebrated again, in the Mystery Plays, the Miracle Plays and then the Moralities. Performed, at first, on Church ground, these seem to have been chanted, and their poetry was a liturgical poetry. Architecture, Painting, Music, Poetry, Dancing and Drama, here, were all one function of Religion. As soon as the performances were taken out of the Church, these conditions changed very quickly. What we call Human Interest began to dominate the Moralities. The abstract virtues and vices, which the actors first presented, became types of personality, characters, humours. The verse was spoken, not chanted, and soon became prose, and the Drama was evolved, Prose Drama,[1] as a distinct form, quite free of any religious function, insulated from the other arts and developing as a self-sufficient entertainment form. It was the field of Democratic Art. Previously, folk art and clerical art had been the

---

[1] Essentially, though it might still be largely in verse. . . . I am distinguishing Prose Drama from Poetic Drama, as that in which the interest is in character, is dramatic, rather than lyrical. The popular stage—in Shakespeare, in Chapman—produced what, by our standards, is the finest Poetry, but Shakespeare's chief theatrical concern was dramatic, not lyrical, and he stands in the tradition of Prose Drama (developing in Dekker, Beaumont and Fletcher, and then directly on, through Congreve and his contemporaries, Sheridan and his contemporaries, to George Bernard Shaw), as opposed to the courtly Poetic Drama, of Lyly, of Peele, whose development links on, here, to that of Opera and Ballet, the lyrical forms. In this period of transition, also, we have figures like Ben Jonson, making the best of both worlds, writing his Humours for the popular stage and then, in later life, giving himself to the production of Masques for polite gatherings, house-parties.

same thing at two levels. Now the people took the Drama to themselves. All the most significant dramatic developments took place, from Marlowe's time, in the popular theatres. Music and Liturgical Drama still developed within the Church, in the Oratorio. But the most significant artistic developments that had Music in their structure became, from religious, polite, which is to say, perhaps, Apollonian, in the most jejune sense.

Music, Dancing and Poetic Drama—all the forms of splendour, which Religion could no longer support, betook themselves to the courts. At first, there also, they existed as one composite form, in Interludes and Masques, which were both sung and played, danced and declaimed. Then spoken verse gradually disappears, and we have musical spectacles, with singing and dancing, which finally split up into the two distinct forms of Opera and Ballet. As these existed at first, in the courts, they were not true art-forms, at all. They were elaborations of court festivities, arranged by the court musicians for balls and banquets, and it was the King and his courtiers, not professional artists, who did the dancing, at least. But the form, if it is to be called a form, had reached a high development before the end of the sixteenth century. For the betrothal of Marguerite de Lorraine and le Duc de Joyeuse, Catherine de Medici had a spectacle prepared, in 1581, which was important enough to be called *Le Ballet Comique de la Reine,* though Ballet Comique was the generic name and though la Reine had had a good many of them, and which was written up and expensively published, the following year, in book form. Its deviser, Baldasarini da Belgiojoso, or Balthazar de Beaujoyeux, Catherine's valet de chambre and head musician, had definite choreographic ideas and viewed his work, in his

Some Beginnings

Preface to the book of it, as a kind of human geometry. He says, also:

'*J'ai animé et fait parler le Ballet, et chanter et resonner la Comédie : et y ajoutant plusieurs rares et riches représentations et ornements je puis dire avoir contenté, en un corps bien proportionné l'oeuil, l'oreille et l'entendement.*'

Around the legend of Circe, he had worked up the Dance, with Music, both vocal and instrumental, and poetic declamation, into a single dramatic entertainment which lasted five and a half hours.

Such entertainments, however, bear very little relationship to Ballet, as we understand it. They were called ballets (Ballet, etymologically, can mean any kind of dancing), but their forms were evolved for the Ballroom, not the Theatre. A technical work on dancing, on Orchesography, was written and published, by Thoinot Arbeau, in 1588, but the forms with which it deals are the courtly forms of Pavane, Courante, Allemande, Gavotte, etc., whose proper performance was a necessary exercise with any person of fashion, a necessary part of Court instead of Church Ritual. Cyril W. Beaumont publishes Thoinot Arbeau's book, now, translated by himself, from his shop in Charing Cross Road. And let me pay, here, my own general tribute to Mr. Beaumont—a form of tribute which becomes almost unnecessary, so inevitably must any writer on any aspect of the Dance pay it—for his votive labours in making everywhere accessible all the most important writings and pictures in the Dance's history. Anybody who wants to study these forerunners of Ballet, in detail, can be fully gratified by way of Mr. Beaumont. For present purposes, it is sufficient that Belgiojoso was an Italian, who brought his work to France. Italy is the great womb of the musical arts, as England is of the verbal arts, and France has been the best nurse of them all. It is to Louis XIV of France, Le Roi Soleil, at any rate, that we owe the beginnings of Ballet proper, in the Theatre.

Himself an enthusiastic dancer, Louis XIV had the services of so great a musician as Lully and so great a dramatist as Molière, for his court entertainments, with choregraphers working in their own right—Beauchamps, Bocan and Pécourt—and even a specialist technician, in Vigarani. It is not generally understood that Molière had considerable importance for the development of Ballet (Ballet, also, of course, for the development of Molière), though, as late as 1924, Boris Kochno and Bronislawa Nijinska got together to work again on a Molière scenario, *Les Fâcheux*, for the Diaghilev Company, with a further revision, by Léonide Massine, in 1927. More important, though, are the facts that, in 1661, L'Académie Royale de Danse was formed, while a school of dancing was added to L'Académie Royale de Musique, in 1672; and that, in performances given by the products of these schools, Ballet was progressively shifted from the Court to the public theatres. The themes were Greek and Roman myths. The dancers were exclusively male. Elaborate masks were worn, and costumes too grand to permit any very agile dancing. And then, in 1681, in *Le Triomphe de l'Amour,* Lully had the Court ladies dance. A repeat performance, for the public, brought in female dancers from the Academy. And Mlle. Lafontaine was installed, in History, as the first true ballerina.

This is the beginning of Ballet proper. From this point, Ballet developed rapidly and has developed continuously. It was freed at last, from its rather false union with sung and spoken words. The process of splitting up sophisticated art into self-sufficient art-forms, a dividing up as of plants, for freer growth, was complete. A group of young intellectuals, met together at the house of Count Bardi, in Florence, had devised the first opera, *Dafne,* in 1597: which had developed, already, by 1608, into the very subtle art of Monteverdi, whose *Orfeo* is still among the finest operatic scores in existence, while Purcell, before the end of the seventeenth century, had created English works fully fit to go with it. By the end of the century, also, Imperial Expansion was in full process; The Royal Society, in England, had drawn men's minds towards the scientific experimentation, the obsession with Technique, which led to the Industrial Revolution, the Machine Age; the bourgeois, the economic individualist, was unmistakably in the ascendant, over the landed gentry, and had already imposed his will, in Civil War, in England and Germany; and the French Revolution was doubtless hoarded up, to work more suddenly and violently, only because France was still a Catholic country, a country which had not accepted Bourgeois Individualism in Religion. It was natural, therefore, that the most significant artistic developments, also, should now take place outside the Court, in the ranks of the rising, the revolutionary class.

In Ballet, at any rate, the eighteenth and early nineteenth centuries present us with a long succession of great dancers, who had some ambiguous royal patronage, certainly, but who came from and appealed to the Bourgeoisie, first and last, and with a development of Technique as rapid and intensive as that of Applied Science. Compare this with the position in the other arts. . . . Poetry and the Drama were now completely separated. The Restoration dramatists, with the end of the Heroic Play, wrote Prose Drama exclusively, starting a direct line (there is a break, in France and Germany, with the Romantic Revival) to Robertson and Pinero. In the Augustan Age, the kinds of Poetry were strictly insulated, and, after Johnson, with Gray and Collins, Poetry came normally to mean Lyric Poetry. The Novel, the most characteristic modern literary form, was evolved, to find almost complete fulfilment in Smollett and Fielding. Pure Music, which was almost unknown before, had grown up in Italy, and within the century, would find its highest manifestations in Bach and Mozart. Painting and Sculpture were quickly becoming self-sufficient forms, set apart from the decorative functions which they had held, even in Renaissance Italy. Glück did all the spadework for the modern kind of Opera, the would-be Music Drama. And, in Ballet, though the basic forms were still the Bourrée, Chaconne, Gigue, Minuet, etc., and though the legs and thighs were not unanimously turned out at ninety degrees until the end of the century, a technical work by R.-A. Feuillet, in 1701, makes a definite formulated art of Choregraphy (conceived entirely in horizontal terms, though), and, about the same time, Pierre Beauchamps schemed out the five positions of the feet.

Which, combined with the turning out at ninety degrees, and with the corresponding positions of the arms, are as important in Ballet as, shall we say, stress or accent is (as opposed to quantitative measure) in European verse. . . . The turning out of the legs and thighs was established as a textbook rule by about 1780, the complete theory of balance for the whole body by 1830, by which date, too, the women dancers were on their points. But the general historical movement, from the beginning of the eighteenth century to the beginning of the twentieth, was a movement towards perfecting the individual dancer, rather than the choregraphic forms of the Dance, and all this technical development was an essential part of the movement. Bourgeois Individualism found itself fully liberated with the Industrial Revolution, at the end of the eighteenth century, to go on simply perfecting and expanding its technique, until it should become a creature of such power that it must necessarily involve itself in chaos, choking itself, and need organisation beyond itself, with its own Will to Power denied. This is also the pattern of Ballet's development. The Dancer was liberated, even from the Decencies: the maillot was countenanced, even in the Papal Theatre, on condition of being dyed blue. There was national commercial enterprise in the Dance, and international competition. One country had to go on evolving more prodigious dancers than another. Before the end of the nineteenth century, the Dancer had become so powerful a machine that nobody quite knew what to do with him.

Here is his immediate lineage. . . . Marie Camargo, who did entrechats quatre, various jetés and the pas de basque and first displayed the female calf, in the Versailles landscapes of Watteau and Fragonard. . . . Marie Sallé, who came over from prudish Paris to lewd London, in 1734, to dance in nothing but corset, petticoat and a piece of muslin. . . . Maximilien Gardel, who dared to throw a temperament at the Opéra, abolished wigs and masks and executed ronds des jambes. . . . Gaetan and Auguste Vestris, the latter of whom (the son) was premier at the Opéra for thirty-five years, rose higher in the air than anyone before him and stayed there longer than anyone since, except Nijinsky (and a certain Damashov): so that his proud father declared, if Auguste did descend to earth,

from time to time, it was purely out of consideration for
the feelings of his less agile colleagues. . . . Marie Taglioni,
who first danced in true moonlight and muslin, about 1830,
and who rose almost as high in the air as Auguste Vestris,
was as highly paid as most film stars, (a hundred pounds per
appearance); she inspired the poet Théophile Gautier to
utterance as extravagant as his red waistcoat . . . . Fanny
Elssler, who counterparted Taglioni, in the more highly coloured, the Victor Hugo part of the Romantic Movement.
. . . Around these, Carlotta Grisi, Lucille Grahn, Fanny
Cerrito, doing an eternal pas de quatre, with Taglioni, in
Chalon's dainty lithograph. . . . And then there was a lull.
Bourgeois Europe had, shall we say, evolved its high-class
standard product in the Dance.

And had exploited it to the full. . . . Balletic enterprise
now covered the whole of Western Europe and began to
present the cartel, combine, syndicate aspect of Industry
in general. Three important theorists of Ballet had arisen.
They were Jean-Georges Noverre, whose *Letters*, of 1760,
still offer as adequate an æsthetic for Ballet—and as ambitious a programme for the Theatre of the Future—as we
have, though Ballet was not fully created in his day, and he
is, therefore, an anachronism, like William Blake; Salva-
tore Viganò, who applied what was immediately practic-
able of Noverre, in a large field, and refined on some aspects of his thought; and Carlo Blasis, who gave us such
characteristic Ballet postures as the 'attitude' (derived
from the *Mercure* of Jean de Boulogne) and drew up the
theory of the port des bras. Noverre took his work to
Stuttgart. Viganò toured Europe and finally settled in
Milan, in 1812. Blasis worked out his thories in an elaborate and important Traité, in 1820, and then, in 1837, be-

took himself, after Viganò, to Milan, where he directed
the Imperial Academy of Dance and Pantomime, at the
Scala. Sallé, as I have pointed out, had had to come to England, to free the Dance of pads, panniers and perukes.
The Napoleonic Wars robbed England, at the century's
turn, of French dancers, but Ballet, by then, was firmly
established, here. We find a London journalist writing,
for June 11, 1835:

'*The ballet of "La Chasse aux Nymphes" followed Bellini's
"Puritani" at the King's Theatre last night. Taglioni was all in
all. What nonsense wiseacres talk when they say there is nothing
intellectual in dancing; let those who think so go and see
Taglioni.*'

And, by the middle of the century, there was no big
European capital city without some Ballet. But Bourgeois
Society cannot go beyond a fine standard article, and
Ballet, to achieve its ultimate perfection, had to isolate
itself from Bourgeois Society.

Ballet, in fact, had to go to the one big European or
partly European country which had not yet had its Bourgeois Revolution: which was still Feudal in its structure,
which had saved up all its forces of change and would have
both its Bourgeois and its Proletarian Revolutions, all at once,
in 1917. Midway through the nineteenth century, Ballet
came to its highest development in Italy, which also was un-
industrialised. And then all forces began to converge on
Russia. French choreographers went North. Scandinavian
teachers went East. And the Italian dancers, lastly, took
over their phenomenal technique to be refined and surpassed in the forcing-houses of the Imperial Schools of
Nicholas I and Nicolas II. In other countries, Ballet was
temporarily left to decline to the music-halls, though, even

here, they maintained the continuity of normal technical development and kept the public's appetite whetted, at the Alhambra and the Empire, from 1871 to the outbreak of the War.

It is commonly agreed that Bourgeois Society, to-day, is tired, and this apparently quite Marxian brief survey of the development of Ballet is likely to be more pleasing to amateur politicians than to amateur æsthetes. What I am most conscious of, myself, however, is the very beautiful historical pattern. That the Dance should reflect the development of Society's conditions so much more clearly than any other art is, I suppose, natural, since the basic substance of the Dance is not words, or notes, or pigments, but the human being, the major unit of society. The Poet, the Musician, the Painter, may all be specimens of the Economic Man. The Dancer is also a commodity. But the development of Bourgeois Society isolated the Dancer, finally, more and more completely, and then, having standardised him at as high a level as possible, shipped him off to Feudal Society, to achieve perfection. So that, as Bourgeois Society becomes finally ridiculous, the Dancer becomes, also, the most obvious contrast to its conditions, though these conditions still obtain in the circumstances under which the Dancer's work is presented.

To the politic-minded, this position of Ballet, as a perfect abstract of Social History, should be enough, in itself, to prove its importance, as opposed to anything more

Plate 1. 1853. Collection Derra de Moroda.

44

easily born and rapidly developed, the mushroom forms of
the Dance. And, to the literary-minded, it should be
enough to contemplate the equally sustained relation of
Ballet with Literature. In their beginnings, the two were
united. After the major split, Ballet took its justification
from Literature. It evolved its forms round themes borrowed from Literature: specifically, from Molière, for instance, and then, more generally, from the classical
legends, the cult of the Ancients, which dominated the
eighteenth century as a whole. The French Revolution
brought in romantic, exotic and patriotic themes. *La Fête
de l'Etre Suprême, La Dansomanie* and a ballet done to the
Marseillaise (all by Pierre Gardel) finally replaced the Cas-
tors and Polluxes, the Titans, the Pygmalions. And then
J.-G. Noverre had furnished Ballet with its own æsthetic,
and the process was reversed. Gautier was inspired by Taglioni (and by the Spanish gypsies). The Dance had more
influence on Literature than Literature had on the Dance.
But the Dance has not—or had not—the same Will to
Power, to absorb all other arts, as Literature has, and, as
soon, almost, as it was established, forsook its position of
ascendancy and went off to the Imperial Court of Russia,
to submit itself patiently to counsels of perfection.

From which the Dancer would emerge, half a century
later (would come spinning and pounding out of the
North), like the ambassador of some divine forgotten race,
to blazon his radiant energies across a very confused and
very sluggish world, about to be helplessly convulsed in the
imbecile monstrosity of the War. . . . But I have simplified the historical pattern, and I have spent a lot of space,
elsewhere, in arguing that to simplify is to falsify, to embrace with a formula is to strangle. Before the creation of

this strange symbolic being, the Dancer, in the fittingly strange atmosphere of the Russian Imperial Schools, there are some minor historical movements to be glanced at, in the Dance, and the activities of some dancers, not spectacular or symbolic enough to be talked of, pseudo-mystically, as embodiments of The Dancer, with capital letters, but important, none the less. Revived Greek, Central European, Dalcroze Eurhythmics, Kurt Jooss and the International Institute of Margaret Morris Movement: these are sophisticated mushroom forms of wisdom and unwisdom, whose handling belongs to the matter of Isadora Duncan. But what are the precedents for that monotonous and monochromatic shuffling, the curious wag and swerve, which so much gladdens and absorbs the beauties and gallants of Kilburn and Oldham, the lasses and lads of Mayfair?

The Science of Orchesography, as studied by Thoinot Arbeau, towards the end of the sixteenth century, concerned itself with the Allemande, Branle, Courante, Galliard, Gavotte, Mauresque, Pavane, Volte: with dance-forms that we look upon as evolved for the Ballroom, not for the Theatre. And these forms, with such later additions as the Minuet, were the basis of all Ballet to the time of Camargo and, in fact (though not so obviously), with the Valse, of nearly all Ballet to the time of Fokine. But these forms were not polite in origin. They are folk-forms. The Dance, basically, is the first spontaneous form of expression of a vigorous people, and, in Western Europe, the common people evolved these forms and gave them to the nobility, who polished and stylised them, made them polite and terre-à-terre, turned the hautes danses into basses danses (for reasons not so much of state as of dress) and then handed them on to the professional dancers, who maintained the stylistic polish of the nobility, but reïnfused, into their precise forms, all the vigour and zest—and Elevation —of their originators. It is a fact which ought to be noticed by your balletomaniac, who is commonly a snob of the most wretched kind, a sort of pseudo-White Russian snob. Arnold Haskell wrote, once, that 'Ballet suffers from its tacit acceptance as something beautiful', and it is a wise remark. But I fancy that Ballet suffers even more from its tacit acceptance as something polite. This, at any rate, is always the order of processes within the Dance: spontane-ous and exuberant creation of forms, sophistication and general lowering of intensity, reïnvigoration.

Or was the order, until the last century. . . . With the Renaissance, an international Christendom split up into self-contained nations; an hierarchical nation into purely economic classes; the single communal focus of creative expression into self-contained art-forms. And there are rigid class-divisions in forms of the Dance, from the same time. But dancing is a matter, first, of coursing blood and urgent muscles, and the blood of one class is only a little more acid, the muscles only a little slighter and stiffer, than those of another. So there is constant interaction of forms. The different cabrioles of Ballet are final versions of the capers which the Elizabethan gentleman cut on the pre-Elizabethan peasant's pattern. But the Elizabethan age was a great age in the creation of dance-forms, as in the creation of all expressive forms. The blood, it seems, coursed freely, then. Shakespeare's Sir Toby Belch wanted to know, of the foolish knight, Sir Andrew Aguecheek, who thought he had 'the back-trick simply as strong as any man in Illyria':

'Why dost thou not go to church in a galliard, and come home

in a coranto? My very walk should be a jig: I would not so much as make water but in a sink-a-pace.'

Ben Jonson lamented:

'*Now the concupiscence of dances and of antics so reigneth, as to run away from nature, and be afraid of her, is the only point of art that tickles the spectators. But how out of purpose, and place, do I name art?'*

And Religion was not yet altogether set apart from the Dance, though the Dance was secular. Thoinot Arbeau himself was a priest: his proper title is Jehan Tabourot, Abbé de Lengres. The satisfactory conclusion of that Renaissance round-table conference, the Council of Trent, in 1553, was celebrated with a ball in which the prelates themselves danced with the red-hot mammas of their day. And even Thomas Nashe's Dick Harvey, at Saffron Walden, 'having preacht and beat downe three pulpits in inveighing against dancing, one Sunday evening, when his wench or friend was footing it aloft on the greene, with foote out and foote in, and as friskin and busie as might be at *Rogero, Baselino, Turkelony, All the flowers of the broom, Pepper is black, Green Sleeves, Peggy Ramsey,* came sneaking behind a tree, and lookt on.'

In later times, too, the Mazurka, the Valse, the Polka, have all come from the common people, have set crazes running in the ranks of the Bourgeoisie and then have furnished Choregraphy with new material for the final, the Ballet forms. At the present day, however, the common people—now better styled plain men and women, perhaps, or Men in the Street—have no more creative vigours than anybody else. Since the Yeoman of England gave place to the Economic Man, the muscles of the West-European masses have evolved no new dance-forms. The Bourgeoisie, therefore, has had to look elsewhere, and the Man in the Street, in his turn, to do the imitation. The pseudo-swamps of the Southern States, the nostalgic moaning and swaying of a slave race by the waters of an industrial Babylon— thinned out and speeded up by New York Jews—have provided us with forms that express, at once, our craving for the Bigger and Better (the Louder and Funnier) and our own despair and partial understanding that we, also, are uprooted and enslaved. This is Jazz. It has given us a new mode of musical consciousness, altogether, and has stopped us dancing. In Harlem, though, where the black exiles have made a new society of their own, creative energies have been unleashed which, however spuriously and in however small scope, have made of the Dance the same religious frenzy that it was in Dionysian Greece and brought its tapping and shuffling, chafing discomfort to forms of great complication, vigour and exhilaration; this we can see and hear when The Blackbirds give us, in one programme, the plangent blues of Duke Ellington, the superb Dionysian tap of Nyas Berry and the sinuous wrapt exotics of Kahloah, which I shall doubtless be thought mad, by reputable balletomaniacs, for describing as major art, though its pale reflections in our own ballrooms—what Aldous Huxley calls 'the imitative copulative article'—are, I must insist, greatly inferior, as dancing, to certain forms of activity which are not recognised as dancing at all.

It may still seem that Ballet—at least, as it is now—is purely an art of the Intelligentsia, since the common man, as a rule, is one of those 'healthy Englishmen shocked to the soul by moonlight and muslin'. And the answer to this, as an objection, is that your common man, rejecting Ballet at one of its levels, is involved, by the richer necessity of his nature, in a zest and feeling for its essentials to which your intellectual reaches only now and again. For instance, I do not know why the common man thinks he goes to a Football match. Nor, I imagine, does he. But I am quite sure that what he finds there is 'human bodies behaving in an unusually lovely manner' and that the particular lovely manner in which they behave is extraordinarily balletic.

This statement is entirely solemn. If violence were the quality sought for, Rugby would be more loved than Association Football, which, in this country, anyway, it is not. And the loyalties, the Local Patriotism involved, are by no means fundamental. Every footballomaniac knows that the team he follows rarely recruits a member from its own home-town. Local Patriotism, in fact, is a trick for rationalising purely dramatic sympathies, for heightening essential dramatic tensions, which are very much more important, in Football, than anything that could properly be called choregraphic tensions. Football, actually, is choregraphically weak, since only those players immediately engaged with the ball are relevant to the plastic structure at all. But the very definite style of Association Football is almost pure Ballet style, and the fact that it originates entirely in usefulness, is a utilitarian style, can only make plain the deep conditioning of Ballet. Apart from the general deftness, speed and clean lines of the game, and apart from the importance of a fine Elevation in play near the goal-mouth, the acts of kicking, heading and breasting the ball involve the finely trained player, often, in formal développés, arabesques and attitudes. More particularly still, not only does the good inside forward tend to 'turn out', in the Ballet sense, to make his dribbling as brilliant as possible, but also, in feinting and avoiding a tackle, he executes quite unmistakable pas de basque, pas de bourrée, pas de chat, and ronds des jambes, both frequently and, sometimes, with excellent precision.

As dancing, all the other games are very much inferior to Association Football. Rugby Football has some lovely movements: in the wheeling forward of a line of three-quarters, with the highly stylised passing of the ball along the line. But it has neither the general deftness and speed nor the variety of movement that dancing must have to be completely satisfying. Cricket is painfully slow, and only the fielders have much serious dancing to do, the batsman's line, for instance, being intolerably weak, most of the time, with the parallel arms at right angles to the bat, except in a few strokes through the slips and leg-glides, which can be very lovely indeed. Tennis, though the most uniformly fast game of them all, and though a good match is choregraphically flawless (the possible range of tensions very much limited, by so few players, and precise in consequence), has very little scope for full style, since the main stress, in every movement, must always be in the racket arm. And so on. . . . Association Football is the highest form of Dance in the Stadium, as Classical Ballet is the highest form of Dance in the Theatre, and the common man has preferred it—for that reason, mainly, we may suppose, whatever reasons he gives himself. He rejects Ballet in moonlight and muslin, but turns out to enjoy it, in his millions, when it wears its equally conventional other garb of striped jerseys and short pants.

A later argument will be that the Dance in general, Ballet in particular, will not fulfil itself altogether until the Theatre and the Stadium are assimilated to each other: a consummation which will also betoken the final health of Society. The end of this book, in fact, is to work out a large communal attitude towards the Dance, as well as to devise what critical standards are needed, now, to keep Ballet in health. Meanwhile, we have a conception of Ballet as, in some way, related to the whole business of living. Sadler's Wells apart, we have one piece of testimony, also, in the tremendous mass draw of the most balletic of organised games, that Ballet for Everyman is not a mere Utopian dream, though Football is, at present, as much commercialised and outwardly debased as Ballet in the Theatre ever was, and your international centre-forward can throw a temperament with the most petted of ballerine.

But a German anthropologist may be needed, to make this bond between Ballet and Football respectable. There actually was one such, then, though I cannot find his name, who did locate the origins of Football in Sacrificial Dance. According to him, the head of the sacrificial goat was believed to have and confer great magical power. And the struggling of the onlookers for its possession, once earnest and doubtless bloody, was later stylised as a piece of Ritual, with a bladder substituted for a skull.

But, reverting. . . . Evidently, with the scope this book has, this historical and geographical survey of the Dance as a whole cannot be made anything like exhaustive, and this very important matter of Jazz, the diametric opposite of Ballet, must be left alone, here; though, one day, somebody will have to make us a separate book out of its enormous musico-choregraphic significances and possibilities. For the moment, it is more important to notice certain other movements in that complex organic process of the European Dance. It has been observed that the central tradition

52

Some Beginnings

of Ballet started in Italy, spread into France, was deflected into England and passed through later important phases in Austria, Germany and Scandinavia, before gathering itself up again and converging on Russia. In these countries, the folk-dance forms were drained off, concentrated in Ballet and left, in themselves and among their originators, as expressions of small importance and very small power. In other countries, where Ballet did not drain off folk-energies, but was imported only lately, very lovely folk-dance forms grew up and have survived.

The First International Folk-Dance Festival, for instance, which was held in London, in July, 1935, a colossal affair that required, for a week, both the Regent's and Hyde Parks and the Albert Hall, gave us magnificent opportunities to make comparison between the rather old-maidenly, rather manufactured and bogus and very, very arts-and-crafts heartiness of the English Morris teams, with their French and German counterparts, and the authentic traditional forms that have come from Hungary, Jugo-Slavia, Poland, Russia, Spain.

This is only the bones of the matter. Anybody who wants the full succulent meat (of this particular hind-part) must go to the admirable writings of Cecil J. Sharp, though he founded the English Folk-Dance Society and was, I believe, a bad anatomist. But the country which has brought the Popular Dance to its evident highest level is Spain. Here, there has been a great conflict of bloods, of Latin, Moor, Romany, Goth and Celt, and a wide range of very complex and very beautiful dance-forms has grown up out of it: Dionysian, certainly, and expressive of an old mystery but—when the people as a whole becomes levelled out to the standard bourgeois level of Europe as a whole and dances Blues, Boston and Fox-trot, instead of Bolero and Jota (even rejecting its own Tango for the American-Jewish form)—producing an Apollonian art, also, in remarkable individual dancers like La Argentina and El Escudero.

A very baldly stylised composite Spanish Dance entered into Ballet, long ago, and was the staple 'character dance' with Petipa. But the balletic possibilities of these powerful fusions of Eastern and Western characters have not been nearly exhausted, although, these last few years, Léonide Massine has derived a great deal from them. Something similar applies to some other forms. After Spain, the place of wildest and loveliest dancing has probably been Hungary. Here, also, there was a strong Romany strain. And a bare version of the Hungarian Czardas has long been used in Ballet (also much exploited by Massine, notably in *Le Beau Danube*): as have the Polish Mazurka and Polonaise and the native Russian Gopak, together with odd bits of nonsensical Chinoiserie and Exotik, from nowhere in particular. But there is still great riches of dancing forms to be got from these folk-expressions and assimilated to Ballet. Last year, for instance, Pio and Pia Mlakar produced, in Zurich, *The Devil in the Village*, a highly successful three-act ballet that used both Jugo-Slavian legend and Jugo-Slavian dance-forms notably the Kola, which, in itself, has seventy-two variations of steps, each of them peculiar to one district.

Yesterday, too, at sundown, the rabbits were dancing in the hay-field. They were doing elaborate circular and processional figures. 'Rabbits play game, you know. A sort of tig. . . .' That was Herbert Read, who is not fond of the Dance. And then, as the moon brightened out, though it was not quite full, innumerable black cats were dancing. One was mimicking and prancing at a moth. Two of them did an eccentric pas de deux, with grotesquely wrapt serenity, against the whitening wall. The smallest of them all was practising original kinds of pirouettes and tours en l'air, in the dark far corner. And all their pas de chat, besides. . . . A bat flapped and hovered, curvetted down, with scudding side-skips along the grass's edge, and then swayed lazily out of sight, across the tarn. All these variations were new, and very old, and all of them were lovely.

B. The Russian School and the Meaning of Tradition

You take, shall we say, the tube to Baron's Court. Round the corner is St. Paul's School. If it is a summer afternoon, hundreds of boys are working at the nets: short and creamy-skinned, long and spotty-faced, agile and skilled or merely strenuous, and some with greying hair who would be masters, not boys, if they were not dressed in whites. There is clicking of bats and thin cries. It is very English. Many of these boys will go into the British Army. The big house is across the way. The bell brings to the door Capt. G. E. Tsapline, D.S.O., D.S.C., with a scar on his cheek and a Slavonic, not an English, military bearing. He bows stiffly. He also smiles. He once captured—so he tells me—a whole battalion of the Red Army, in the Counter-Revolution. He trained machine-guns on them, counted them up—exactly six hundred and thirty-seven men—and shot them down. The house belongs to The North Russian Association. On the hall-stand are letters addressed to famous dancers, who are dancing at Covent Garden. Inside is a portrait of His Imperial Majesty Nicolas II. It is very White Russian. Many of the girls and boys who come here will go to Paris.

Legat's studio is on the first floor. Formerly there were two studios, both enormous, but they were turned into a private theatre (last year), so that one wall is a stage and a proscenium arch and a big maroon curtain. A great mirror stands in front of the stage, and two grand pianos in the corners. There are the long windows of the conservatory, where rows of red plush chairs are stored and which can become a refreshment bar. The rest of these other three walls is covered with photographs and caricatures of dancers, and, at the back of the room, there is the big, blue and hideous original of Serov's Pavlova poster for the Diaghilev Company's first appearance in Paris in 1909. There is an oil painting, also, of Legat, and a bronze bust of him. Mothers of dancers—a devoted and anxious folk—are sitting on both sides the mirror, against the stage. Girls in black or pink tights and all kinds of odd upper garments are coming in and kissing each other and everybody else (which they would not do in St. Paul's School, across the way). A few are already limbering and stretching themselves into incredible shapes along the bars. And the little shaven-headed man, in the centre, who potters about with a pale-blue watering-can, sprinkling the floor, smiling, looking up to make impossible jokes to the mothers, in quite incomprehensible English, is Nicolas Legat himself, former

Plate 2. 'The Unholy Trinity' by Nicolas Legat. *Left to right:* Edwin Evans, Arnold L. Haskell and P. J. S. Richardson. *By kind permission of M. Nicolas Legat.*

N.LEGAT.

THE UNHOLY TRINITY OF THE CAMARGO SOCIETY

The Russian School and the Meaning of Tradition

Master of The Russian Imperial Ballet, teacher of Karsavina, Pavlova, Fokine, Nïjinsky, Massine, Dolin, among many others only a little less well known.

His gait, with the strongly out-turned hips, declares, at once, a life's submission to the Ballet discipline. His evident health and good humour declare, equally, that growing old has not meant retirement from the service of Ballet, and this may be noted as one difference between Ballet and Athletics: that the athlete grows fat in later life, and so, I believe, do most non-Ballet dancers. Anyway, all the dancers duly kissed, and the floor well-sprinkled, the girls (the boys, if there are any) go to their places at the bars, their Maestro to the piano. He improvises. He does not read music. He feels that also, with all his art, in muscular terms: a pure relation between fingers and keys. The caricatures on the walls, too, which are all his. . . . Their feeling is for the muscular characters of his victims, rather than a purely visual simplification. The pupils stand with feet apart—second position—and one hand lightly on the bar. Pliés, first, to loosen the legs and prevent stiffness, and then the various grands et petits battements, to loosen more positively and to sharpen the feet for these seemingly impossible little beats we call entrechats. . . . This practice at the bar goes on for twenty minutes or so, with fouetté turns, développés, various other adages. And then the pupils come out into the centre, the most advanced in front: Anna Roje foremost, always, and, if it is a good day, dancers as good as Kyra Nijinsky and the very beautiful Pearl Argyle in the front line proper. Postures like those at the bars are gone through here, too, becoming more complicated and strenuous, making the pupils pant and sweat already. And then they resin their shoes on a tray at the back of the room and come crowding round the piano, while Legat shows increasingly difficult and very lovely enchaînements of steps, with his fingers and interlocking hands on the piano top.

You are amazed that these young dancers can respond to the instructions and carry out the difficult enchaînements with so little faltering, not only rightly, but with an immediate and almost creative feeling, also, for their stylistic flow. You hear them make a few remarks to each other, as they crowd round the piano, and you observe that, for the most part, they are green and silly girls. Yet they receive at once and project into swift concrete forms an idea that you have to watch for, time and time again, before you begin to understand its complication. You probably coin some such phrase as 'intelligent bodies', to account for the phenomenon. And it is a just one. What Mind is, what Body is, and how the two interplay, is a problem that has always perplexed philosophers, and it comes to a very sharp focus in the Dance. Watch Legat. He says very little. His fingers dance on the piano top and then on the piano keys. His pupils expand the pattern his fingers have made, to the pattern of sound his fingers are making. He utters a few short, technical, purely denotative phrases, with a few private jokes intermixed. But he knows, has troubled to learn, has needed to learn, very little English and only the French technical terms. Speech, the apparatus of the Mind, is almost superfluous. For the most part, the day's lesson goes through in a wrapt uncanny mindless silence. Legat has devised and published elaborate systems, which are used everywhere. But, in this infinitely complicated process, by which ideas evolved through centuries are renewed and transmitted from Maestro to pupils, from the Russian Imperial

The Russian School and the Meaning of Tradition

Schools to the youngest generation of English dancers, growing, producing more and more difficult, swift and compelling forms, there is very little intervention of what we commonly mean by Mind.

Sitting at the piano, with gestures that can seem commonplace, Nicolas Legat, the person, embodies in himself, radiates, or transmits in some other half-mystical way, and at the same time increases, sharpens, purifies, the whole course of the human body's creative history in the Modern World. He took the science of Choregraphy from Marius Petipa, the science of Pedagogy from Christian Johanssen, and preserved them both, alone, till Fokine came along, and the Diaghilev Company, to take the Art of Dance out into Western Europe. He has a history which goes back through Taglioni, the Vestris, Camargo, Sallé, Noverre, Lafontaine, the Abbé de Lengres, and back much further, in a more blurred perspective. His own immediate family heritage goes back more than a century, in Russia, though his origin is not Russian. His history is, at least, the whole history of the Russian School, and the Russian School is a focus for all that had preceded in France, Italy, England, Scandinavia, where Ballet's course had been continuous since the Renaissance. We can except the writings of Valerian Svetlov, a non-dancer, perhaps the only one who ever knew very much about dancing, but, otherwise, Legat's own accounts, as he has written them down and as I have had them from him (in our two or three dozen common words of English, French and Russian and by Anna Roje's and Capt. Tsapline's interpretations), are about the only satisfactory accounts of that phase of Ballet's history which represents, surely, the oddest and the most powerful phenomenon in all art's development.

Moonlight and Muslin

Legat is Scandinavian by origin. So was Christian Johanssen. The pedagogic bases of the Russian School were Scandinavian. Johanssen came to St. Petersburg as a mere boy, though, in the first quarter of the nineteenth century. And Legat's grandfather and great-uncle, Ivan and Samuel Legat, before him, had organised the best of the Balagani, the People's Theatres, in St. Isaac's Square and the Field of Mars, St. Petersburg, and were invited into the Russian Imperial Ballet by Nicolas I himself. Ivan Legat's wife was Constance Lede, a French dancer, and it was their son, Gustav Legat, who first brought Russian blood into the family. Gustav Legat shows us, more clearly, perhaps, than anyone else, the deliberate self-immolation, the strain of pure physical masochism, of which every good dancer surely needs something. Exercises at home, four miles' walk to school, work by himself at the bar, full general practice with Petipa, full general class with Johanssen, four miles back home, more exercises there and so to bed, sleeping always on his back, his feet wedged into the sides of the bed, instep upwards, to help the turning out. . . . He could hold a développé with a boy sitting on his foot or, in the second position, with a full glass of water balanced on the inside of his heel. In a performance of *Russian and Ludmilla*, in a part which he did not like, in a processional figure, Gustav Legat turned out his feet so far that they pointed backward, and the corps, taking their lead from him, turned about and set off marching in the opposite direction, which upset the performance considerably.

This man drilled his two sons, Nicolas and Sergei, into the Imperial Schools, with Didelot scholarships, at a very early age, so that they were mature, almost, with the generation before them. Sergei Legat, the younger of the two, seemed likely to become the best classical dancer of his day. He did some choreography with his brother, and he was an equally accomplished caricaturist. Several collections of their caricatures (at the first suggestion of Igor Stravinsky's father) were published, or exhibited, or sold to the Court balletomaniacs, and would have been a great source of income, but for a publisher who decamped with a good many thousand roubles. Lost in the Revolution, they are now mostly kept in the Bakhrushin Museum, in Moscow. But there is a book of Nicolas Legat's drawings published in London, and dozens of them in the studio, and hundreds at home, these last (done during a long illness) all strained into a muscular grotesquerie which makes them supremely interesting to a student of Ballet, but which would make them rather unappetising in public reproduction. If the two brothers had been able to mature together, in a constant inseparability, there is no supposing what work they might have done. But Sergei Legat cut his throat with a razor in 1905, at the age of twenty-eight, for love, it is said, of Marie Petipa, who was twenty years his senior.

Like many another major dancer, Nicolas Legat paid his way through the Imperial Schools with a Didelot scholarship, and that gives us a starting point for the chronology of the schools. Didelot and Perrot were the first French masters of the Russian Imperial Ballet. That was at the beginning of the nineteenth century, and the Court still recruited its dancers from the private troupes of the landed gentry. By the time Marius Petipa came, the schools had taken a shape. Petipa's father had been Master before him. We find Marius dancing *Giselle*, with Carlotta Grisi, in Paris in 1841. He came to Russia in 1847, uninvited. His brother Ivan had been invited, through their father, from

Marseilles, but Marius arrived first and stole the post of premier danseur, becoming maître de ballet, also, eleven years later. Christian Johanssen was already at work. He was Professor of the schools for some sixty years, and Petipa was Master during most of that time, working under four emperors and up to the time of formation of the Diaghilev Company. Under these two, the Imperial Schools and the Imperial Theatres—one structure—became a monastery of the Dance, airtight forcing-houses with an unflagging discipline not paralleled anywhere, in which all manifestations of ordinary human life seem oddly pathetic. I have the image of a large square well-ventilated artificial womb, or incubator, in which quaintly exuberant and powerful figures move about like the sub-human creatures of *Petrouchka,* enjoying their grotesque loves and practical jokes and suffering their comical agonies with no significance in the outer world but that of their uncontrollable superhuman dancing, seen through a white electrical film.

Christian Johanssen lived to the age of ninety-four, when he could still think to run upstairs, two at a time, and laugh down at the slow Petipa, five years his junior. His wife died just a month before him. In Legat's words:

'*His life-long companion in the flesh, he could not bear being parted from her for a moment, even in death, and at night he stole into the chamber where she lay to fondle her cold face. Coming out he struck his head against the doorpost and brought on a stroke of paralysis. I shall never forget calling on him next day. The stroke had in some way affected his vocal organs and he was unable to speak. He seized his chin with his hand and worked it angrily up and down to indicate the misfortune that had come upon him.*'

And, within a month, he was dead. It all seems curiously

incorrect or, as a novelist would have it, strangely unreal. The reality was Johanssen teaching and the fact that he taught until the year of his death. He himself was a pupil of the Bournonvilles, who had been pupils of Gaetan Vestris. Even in Pedagogy, then, the basic endowment was French. But it was the Swedish Johanssen and then the Swedish Legats who founded, with the endowment, an imperishable science. Which, however, did not permit mere routine. . . . It was Cecchetti, later, who made a closed system of the classical training, with 'a sort of menu of exercises for the week' on the classroom wall. The Russian method was—and, in Nicolas Legat, for one, still is—superior, in that it never allowed the training to go stale, but invented, continually, letting the mind work, as well as the body, at new and increasingly varied enchaînements of steps, which is the true science. Old Russian balletomaniacs have declared that, in sixty continuous years of teaching in Russia, Johanssen never gave two lessons alike.

This inhuman singleness of purpose, then, is the reality, not the human comedy. And the direct Johanssen method is still with us. Nicolas Legat was set to teaching by Johanssen himself, some time before his death. Here, again in Legat's own words, the supreme reality of the Russian School, the concrete and visible handing on of the tradition. . . .

'*At the first few lessons Johanssen sat by my side. Extreme age could not dampen his ardour for his life-work nor his desire to see it worthily continued. At the age of over ninety his sight began to fail him, his vision narrowed, he could see clearly only what was straight ahead of him, and was obliged to turn his head to follow the object he wished to see. I felt there was something profoundly impressive, something tragic, in the situation : this old, old professor*

63

sitting beside me, his chosen pupil, more than sixty years his junior, transmitting to me his wisdom, anxiously guiding my every act, jealously following my every word, my every command. "Enough of that movement," he would say, "now give them this one . . ." and so on. I was intensely nervous with the nervousness of reverence. To me the old man was the deity of the dance. With all my heart and all my soul I desired to hear his blessing: "Well done, good and faithful servant."

'*But Christian Johanssen rarely said as much as that at a time. His highest praise usually was, "Now you may perform in public." So when at the end of the first class he said to me: "Good. You can go on," I knew I had justified his hopes. He came to two or three more classes, but his corrections and comments became fewer and fewer. At his last visit he sat in silence. Only at the end he grunted: "Good." And I know that when he died a few months later he died satisfied.*'

And through the class, as Nicolas Legat held it, passed Matilde Kchessinskaya, Vera Trefilova, Tamara Karsavina, Lydia Kyasht, Michel Fokine, Adolf Bolm, Vaslav Nijinsky. Who did not?

'*The future ballerinas would enter like fairies, tripping lightly, impeccably attired in ballet-skirts of various hues, etherially beautiful. After them would come the men-dancers, bold and energetic, eager to bear their goddess-like partners sky-wards.*'

But who would not be, in the place where it was such a sanctified act? It is unfortunate, I think, that the teaching methods of Enrico Cecchetti should have come into wider use than those of the Russian School proper. They are simpler, it is true, and more easily assimilated, and there-fore, perhaps, more generally fitted to a hurried commer-cial age, and Cecchetti's bequest to the Russian School was, in any case, great. But Johanssen had already assimilated and refined on and largely superseded his work, and Cecchetti training, at the present day, produces dancers in a style noticeably inferior to the style of those produced by the heirs of Johanssen.

A certain stiffness of the upper body and hands that are allowed no phantasy. . . . Enrico Cecchetti came to Russia, with a good many other Italian dancers, in the eighties and nineties of last century. He was needed. The Russian School had not yet acquired the phenomenal acrobatic technique of the Italians. Taglioni and Grisi had already delighted Russia. Virginia Zucchi came next, dancing at a suburban music-hall outside St. Petersburg and then in the Imperial Theatres, in the Hermitage, the Winter Palace and the Mariinsky. She was followed by Brianza, Delera, Grimaldi, Legnani, Limido, with Coppini as Master and Cecchetti as the group's only male dancer. He was in his forties at the time, a small man who did eight pirouettes, when the best Russians were content with four. As a teacher, he was given the 'parallel' class, for girls only, and St. Petersburg was dominated, for a time, by his and his companions' displays of pure virtuosity. It was Legnani who, first appearing in Petipa's *Zolushka*, came to the centre of the stage, at a sudden pause in the coda, and amazed this world by performing thirty-two fouettés on the spot. There are pure-minded æsthetes and æsthetic moralists who are still outraged by thirty-two fouettés. It has nothing to do with art, they say, but only with Acrobatics and the attendant vulgarities. True. . . . But there is a curious exhilaration about it, a power which may not be the power of plastic beauty but is no less compelling on that account.

That the stupid and ungainly human body should be able

to turn itself into both top and whip is not only remarkable. It is also highly admirable, even awe-inspiring, an absurdity which can properly be called sublime. The first achievement of thirty-two fouettés was a sign of the Dancer having reached a certain level of stylistic perfection with ease and superfluous energy enough to allow him to begin a display of incredibly pure virtuosity within the stylistic framework. It was the structure of the Dance forming in such richness and organic strength that it could afford to spend itself in putting out irrelevant freak flowers and mad leaves. And, for that matter, the feat can be used for the purposes of great art. Modified, built around, it is the focus of Balanchine's *Cotillon*, sending the whole stage hurling round its maelstrom pillar of attraction, at the close, in a movement by which the movement of El Greco's picture of Jesus and the money-changers is rudimentary. But reverting. . . . The Russians also set themselves to do thirty-two fouettés. At first they could not, though the feat is now within the power of any true ballerina. It was Legat who first taught one of the Russians. He had been partnering Legnani. His miraculous eye saw how Legnani held this and that muscle. And he soon had Matilde Kshessinskaya's body behaving in the same extraordinary fashion, much to the gratification of 'a certain very exalted personage'.

In every way, though, the Russians absorbed and purified and surpassed the work of the Italians. It seems that, in Russia, Ballet had found not only the necessary social conditions but the only right temperament, also, for this historical phase. As Adrian Stokes will have it:

'*It is the situation of renascence . . . the clarification of nor-*

thern fervour by the settled forms and comprehensive style that are
in essence a product of the South.'

Though the process might be more justly stated, perhaps,
in reverse and though it is by no means sure that we 'want
ballet still to be Russian ballet', exclusively. . . .

  '*In the case of Russians, as well as an extreme hyperborean*
element, there is something exotic and Oriental that is clarified by
ballet. . . . As for the hyperborean element, the intense Russian
snows, the whirling flakes that fall so lightly, make an image that
is pleasant to have in mind when watching classical ballet. And
I have little doubt that the snows of Russia have had a profound
influence upon the noted elevation of Russian dancers. One can
well imagine Theatre Street in St. Petersburg, that highly col-
oured street in which was situated the Imperial ballet school, a
street built by the Italian architect, Rossi. Within these Italianate
rooms the hyperborean dancers flew like their native snows.'

At any rate, double tours en l'air, entrechats huit, six or
seven pirouettes, soon became normal to the young generation of Russian dancers. Sergei Legat did fourteen pirouettes at one stroke. Cecchetti was too set to change, and he
could do his spins and pirouettes in only one direction. He
was a vain man and an irascible man, and it was a favourite
cruelty of the young Russians, with their more balanced
training, to goad him into trying to imitate their own series
of double spins in alternate directions. And as to pure acrobatics. . . . There was a young Moscow dancer, a certain
Nicolas Petrovitch Damashov, who never danced out of
Russia. On a visit, Cecchetti wished to show the young
man how to leap. He wet his finger, sprang up in the air
and made a finger-mark high on the classroom wall. Damashov obediently followed and made his finger-mark about
two feet higher. But this Damashov was an amazing crea-

67

ture, altogether, it seems. Nijinsky could leap, and he had the appearance of defeating the laws of gravity, remaining in the air, a moment, at the highest point of his leap. Damashov had the appearance of doing two leaps: one taking off from the ground and one, again, taking off from the previous highest point of ascent. This phenomenon could do an entrechat huit, ascending, and come down with motionless legs. Or he could ascend with motionless legs and do his entrechat huit on the downward journey. He could be doing a single entrechat huit while Nicolas Legat was doing three, and the conductor used to have to hold pauses in the music, at every ascent, when Damashov was dancing. He could also cover the stage of the Moscow Grand Theatre, which was as big as the stage of La Scala, Milan (about twice the size of the Covent Garden stage), in three leaps, feet together, corner to corner.

Unless we are dreaming. . . . However, it was Style, not pure acrobatic Technique that the Russians most worked for and achieved. Nothing can belittle the Italian endowment. But it is a fault that Cecchetti pedagogic methods should have survived the Russian improvements, in general use. Cecchetti ended with Technique. Style, with strict Cecchetti pupils, is an angular efficiency, with an obstinately one-sided momentum and often dreadful faults of shouldering. By the end of the nineteenth century, Christian Johanssen had evolved and handed on, through Nicolas Legat and some others (Kshesinskaia and Preobrajenskaia, notably), an array of dancing forms which we have not yet learnt to handle, choreographically, to the full, but still tend to baulk and evade, in favour of easier effects. In Marius Petipa, however, who was Master till just before his death, in 1910, there was a great choreographer working in the closest and most constant union with Johanssen, and, through him, through Johanssen's pedagogic heirs and through the cumbrous but indispensable notations of Nicolas Sergeiev, very little has been directly lost. In Imperial Russia, in the collaboration of Johanssen and Petipa, we have that most absolute unity between Classroom and Theatre which must always be the ideal in Ballet, if not—with a difference—in all major art-forms.

Petipa did not give lessons. Johanssen never produced a ballet. But their work was shared, in the minutest detail. Petipa's own speciality, as a dancer and, therefore, to some extent, as a choregrapher, was 'character' dancing, the stylised Spanish, in particular, which Petipa had studied—like Massine, later—in Spain. His power to handle masses effectively in the new Ballet terms, also, however, was extraordinary, for he had no substantial precedents, and his pas de deux and his women's solos are still among the most perfect compositions we can know. For the men's solos, however, Petipa borrowed, invariably, from Johanssen, from his class enchaînements. He would sit through Johanssen's classes, with pencil and notebook, and Johanssen, at the end (five years Pepita's senior), 'would wink and say: "The old man's pinched some more" '. But let me insist, at rather greater length, on the necessity, at all times, for this kind of continuity in the creation of choregraphic forms.

That there can be no great Ballet without it, or, more exactly, no sustained tradition of great Ballet. . . . To evolve new forms of bodily movement is, in the Classroom, a natural and an inevitable thing, if the particular teacher is one great enough to be working all the time on a dynamic muscular sympathy, discriminate and cohesive, with his pupils. To evolve new forms of bodily movement, for the Theatre, on the basis of a mental structure, a verbal structure, the libretto, or a purely visual idea, is unnatural. The final theatrical structure must be an elaboration, a welding together, a final statement, of the more spontaneously generated pedagogic forms. There is little likelihood of great ballets coming from any choregrapher who is neither a great teacher himself nor in daily intercourse with a great teacher. Working under other conditions, he will either care little for true dance forms and play for extraneous theatrical effects, or he will be too abstract; will, that is to say, project mental forms and impose them on the body, an order which implies a perverted generative process. Léonide Massine, for instance, does both these things, as will be evident when we come to the analysis of his work. And it seems likely that contact between choregrapher and teacher, as two distinct persons, rather than as two capacities of one person, is the ideal condition.

It seems, in fact, that there must be a gap, for the spark to leap across. Johanssen did no choregraphy for the Theatre, but his importance for Choregraphy was as great as Petipa's. Petipa's importance largely depended on Johanssen's. What Legat's choregraphy was like, when he was both Professor and Master in Russia, from 1908 to 1914 (after refusing Diaghilev's invitations, not to mention Isadora Duncan's), I do not know. None of his ballets survive. But I know that, as teacher only, his creative powers were such that Petipa, still in his prime, had him set the most troublesome pas de deux, some of which still pass under Petipa's name, along with some of the work of Petipa's understudy, Ivanov. And I know that there is more brilliant choregraphy to be seen in one hour, every morning, at the

Legat Studios than there is in two hours, most evenings, at Covent Garden (judged quantitatively, of course, for the Classroom cannot evolve, in itself, the final theatrical perfection of a *Sylphides* or a *Cotillon*). Yet, when Legat comes to compose dances deliberately, as he has done for various shows, since the studios were converted, his choregraphy is quite commonplace and often very thin stuff. He is working, then, on the abstract, the quasi-literary basis, which is the great bane of all Ballet to-day, now that the Russian School is no more, but has been replaced by more or less closely formed touring or drifting companies, drawn from dozens of schools, all over the world.

Leading, if we follow out the line of argument, to the conclusion that organisations like our own resident ballets, the Rambert Ballet and the Vic-Wells Ballet, though, at present, far less well-equipped, are likely, in the long run, to prove more fertile than bigger organisations like the Diaghilev Company and the present de Basil Company. . . . But this section is supposed to be historical, not a study in absolute dialectics. And the vital historical fact, here, is that, in the time of those amazing specimens of longevity and industry, Petipa and Johanssen (apart from countless opera ballets and divertissements, Petipa composed fifty-four full-sized ballets, fifty of which are kept in the attic), Europe had evolved its Art of Dance, both Technique and Style, to a point at which the problem of its application became the single urgent problem. It is a style of almost infinite variety, and it allows for plenty of virtuosity and acrobatics, for a great contrast of styles, too, between the dainty lady and the spinning pounding robustuous male. But it is focused most clearly in that display of pure forms, the classical Adagio, with its following solo variations, where the speed, which Ballet alone has, among forms of the Dance, is newly affirmed and given new meanings.

It is, in fact, a style which embodies all the qualities, of sheerness, sharpness, breadth and clarity, that the West seems always to demand from its achieved forms of art. But let me quote fragments of more of Adrian Stokes's brilliant ornamental proses, bearing on the Adagio from the second act of *Le Lac des Cygnes*, Petipa's master-work.

'*The ballerina is showing the many gradual planes of her body in terms of harmonious lines. While her arms and one leg are extended, her partner turns her slowly round upon the pivot of her straight point. She is shown to the world with the utmost love and grace. She will then integrate herself afresh, raise herself on her points, her arms close to her body . . . . her feet close together, the one slightly in front of the other. It is the alighting of the insect, the shutting of wings, the straightening into the perpendicular of feelers and wings. Soon she will take flight and extend herself again. . . . She seems scarcely to rest upon the ground. She is, as it were, suspended just slightly above the earth so that we may see her better. She seems cut off from the sources of her being, or rather, those dark internal sources are shown by her as something light and white, brittle as are all baubles. . . . The grosser implications of movement fall clear from the sheen and brilliance of the ballerina's technique. The icy refractions, the scintillations from Tchaikowsky's score, powdered, as it were, delicately with snow, suggest her*

Plate 3. *Aurora's Wedding*. (La Belle au Bois Dormant.) En attitude, preparatory to an accumulation of successive and concerted double fouetté turns. *Left to right:* Vera Zorina, Nathalie Branitska, Alexandra Danilova, Tamara Toumanova, Olga Morosova, Tamara Grigorieva. *Malcolm Dunbar Photograph.*

passions and suggest that they are rarefied and vertiginous. More than once the swan princess will fall extended as if in a faint. . . . One impression from so many movements and attitudes that have been prevalent, from heads inclined towards breasts, from over-lapping hands, from undulating arms, from torsos that are curved, from arms raised aloft with their hands and fingers like daffodil cups or like the undersides of the feet of birds in flight, from the repeated pirouettes upon the point in the pas de deux *which now rise before us cylindrical as a swan's neck, from the varied leg-beats and the proud and graceful extension of the body in* arabesque. . . .*But this time she leans back, she stretches higher. Without a trace of hauteur the full sensitiveness of the neck, the softness of the feathers is generously proposed. Movements of infinite undulation underlie her candid form.'*

And the confusion of images, the impotence of this very sensitive language to touch the style more intimately than at the tangent of breath-bated sly erotic yearnings, guarantees the power of the style and its wholly self-integrated, self-contained and anti-literary richness.

It is generally agreed that Ballet was in the state called Decadence at the beginning of the present century, and it is one of many very naïve agreements which our critics and historians seem unable or unwilling to disrupt. Isadora Duncan roused up a sleeping art. Diaghilev gave it life and strength. And so on. . . . The simple truth is that, just as Ballet had needed, historically, to isolate itself in the Russian forcing-houses, to reach the final solution of a single technical and stylistic problem, so, now, it had to spread itself, again, over the whole of Europe, to be set in contact with a wider range of cultural events, to attempt to solve its present problems of extension and application. It was not that Ballet had come to 'a dead end'. It was simply that

Moonlight and Muslin

Ballet needed a change of status, a change in the social conditions in which it was to be presented: to become a more democratic art. In the meantime, like the chaste young lady, it was 'waiting'. It was being preserved and consolidated by such as Nicolas Legat, while Bakst, Benois, Diaghilev and Fokine were busy tidying up their restive minds in the columns of the Russian highbrow journals. The themes of the ballets of this time are negligible, certainly, from a literary point of view, as a list of the titles of Legat's ballets shows well enough in itself: *The Fairy Doll*, *Barbe Bleue*, *Les Quatre Saisons*, *Two Thieves*, *Puss in Boots*, *The Purple Flower*, *The Prince's Enchanted Dream*, *Rose of Marghita*, *The White Lily*, *Kermesse*, *Le Talisman*, *The Khan's Dream*, *La Chasse de Diane*, *Nymphes et Satyrs*. And the standard of decorative art seems to have been very bad baroque. But good music had already been brought in. Tschaïkowsky's music for Ballet, for *La Belle au Bois Dormant*, *Casse-Noisette*, *Le Lac des Cygnes*, is radiant stuff, while, in Glazounov (whatever we may think of his quality now), the work of one still considered revolutionary had been used, both by Petipa, already, in *Raymonda*, and by Legat, in *Les Quatre Saisons*. And the array of dancers ready for exportation and continued home consumption was certainly incredible. Egorova, Karsavina, Kshessinskaya, Kyasht, Varvara Nikitina, Pavlova, Preobrajenskaia, Sedova, Spessivsteva, Trefilova, Bekéfy, Fokine, Paul Gerdt, Theodor Koslov, Mordkine, Nijinsky, Oboukhov, Volinine, are a few of those whose names are still a legend.

So many of whom were Legat's pupils. . . . Compare the picture I did at the beginning of the chapter with this, by the English diplomat, Sir Paul Dukes, K.B.E., of a performance at the Mariinsky, in January, 1914.

The Russian School and the Meaning of Tradition

'It was one of those occasions for which it was quite impossible for any but the most influential to procure tickets, but M. Tartakoff, the director of the Theatre and a good friend, relaxed so far as to allow me to stand just inside of the door of the centre aisle. The audience was composed of the élite of the Russian nobility. The place blazed with jewels and uniforms. The strains of the National Anthem sounded, everyone rose, and all eyes were fixed on the Imperial box as the Tsar, the Tsarina, and the Imperial family entered and took their places. The orchestra, under Richard Drigo, broke into the overture and the curtain rose on the ballet Esmeralda. It was a gala night, but it was also more than that, it was a jubilee night. One by one the chief artists emerged to meet with warm receptions—the beautiful Matilde Kshessinskaya as Esmeralda, the dignified Paul Gerdt as Frolo, the celebrated mime Stukolkin as Quasimodo. Then about half way through the first act, a slight figure in a green jerkin, the poet Gringoire, was dragged on the stage by brigands. Suddenly the performance came to a stop. The entire auditorium rose to its feet. Even the Tsar stood. On the stage the performers deserted their positions to acclaim their colleague, who remained in the centre bowing incessantly, clearly moved to tears by this acclamation.

'The poet Gringoire was Nicolas Legat, and the occasion the celebration of his jubilee of twenty-five years' service in the Imperial Theatre. The demonstration, which lasted a good fifteen minutes, and was repeated again in the next two acts, was a tribute of public admiration. In the last act, tables were brought on and piled with gifts and presents, while the hero of the day received address after address from countless organisations. One telegram read:

> 'Terpsichora tiem bogata
> Shto ti nam dala Legata

Moonlight and Muslin

Such a picture will not be presented again, for all Mr.
Stokes's pleasant and almost convincing phantasies about 'a
distinguished audience'. It is not necessary that it should.
The social conditions permitting it are destroyed or, where
they do persist, in diluted forms, linger on unwelcomely.
But the essential things continue. In the Fulham studios to
which Nicholas Legat came, at last, after being forced out
of Russia, in 1922, we can still see, concretely, how every
young dancer, stretching his legs, refining his gestures,
sweating and poising his body at the bar, is, in the most
literal sense, the incarnation of a Tradition which, though
brought to its sharpest focus only late in the nineteenth
century, goes back many centuries.

Tradition meaning something much more definite and
useful in the Dance than in other fields. . . . Very odd
conditions of Society had been developing, in Western
Europe, while Ballet was reaching its first perfection, in
isolation, in the feudal social structure of Imperial Russia.
Some statement of these conditions has already been adum-
brated, but the most satisfying single image of this modern
world is, I fancy, one of John Middleton Murry's.

'*The earth-tremors of which men are dimly and variously conscious are the grumbling, menacing summons of the Machine that
men should develop a new intelligence, a new awareness, a new
morality, if they are not to be crushed by the Machine. . . . The*

social body which is the earthly substance of Shakespeare's world was a comely, organic and natural thing. We feel it, we know it. It is a world growing with a natural order. Head and limbs are in vital harmony with one another. Suddenly, by the machine, the whole harmony of human life was subverted. As it were in a single night, the sheer muscular strength of the social organism was multiplied a thousand-fold. Suddenly, this comely, organic, natural body of mankind became a monstrosity; the hands and limbs and thews were grown vast and colossal, yet the head remained what it was before. The transformation was fearful. Gestures which used to have a fierce animal grace and beauty, like war, became nightmarish and hideous. The brain, which was once the brain of a healthy, natural man, by the mere fact that it had not changed, became the brain of an idiot. And that great idiot, with the tiny head and the huge limbs, is the true image of a nation to-day. . . . And that great idiot, which is a modern nation, can think of nothing to do with its huge limbs but use them murderously. There is nothing else it can do with them, since to move at all by the old habits is to move murderously. Murderous motion is its only motion, so long as that monstrous parody of an organic relation between the tiny head and the giant body is unchanged. Either the head must grow capable of controlling the body, by finding in itself room for thoughts of a new kind and creating in itself the tissue to be the vehicle of those thoughts; or the body will ignore and deny the head altogether. Either the head must govern the body, or the body will govern the head. Then, the body will cast out of the head the faint remnants of potential change, annihilate the last vestiges of the ideal and the imagination, as it is doing in Germany to-day. Germany is merely the first of these monstrous bodies which has elected to live totally without a mind, rather than endure that revolutionary development of the brain which is the unescapable price of a new organic wholeness, a new natural community. Germany is merely the first of the monstrous bodies to choose to be wholly monstrous.'

That this pattern of being obtains, also, in the microcosmic World of Ballet, I have already suggested and shall develop in my last chapter. Choreography, still, the brain, is not able to cope with the multitudinous forms of the new body of the Dancer. In this, Ballet reflects the total condition of Society (into which it had now to venture), as any art always must. But the contrary fact is of rather more importance, here: that Ballet, in the sense it can give to that slippery concept, Tradition, provides something of a counteragent, an antiseptic, to this condition of things.

In which it is natural that sensitive minds, in their bewilderment, should seek for some permanency, a Frame of Reference, an ordering of Reality Pictures, some continuous under-meaning in the historical process. . . . Tradition is a word that has been discussed quite inordinately much, in this century, especially since the War, which was a great final disruptor of some traditions. It is felt that to establish a full meaning for Tradition—and establish forms of living in the pattern of that meaning—is itself valuable. It is felt, perhaps, that a true consciousness of Tradition could give men the power of governance, 'the brain' in Mr. Murry's image, which this monstrous modern world calls for. In the general cultural field, a statement made by T. S. Eliot, our most widely influential poet, is probably the most satisfactory statement for Tradition, as well as the most widely acknowledged.

'The existing monuments form an ideal order among themselves, which is modified by the introduction of the new (the really new) work of art among them. The existing order is complete before the new work arrives; for order to persist after the supervention of

novelty, the whole existing order must be, if ever so slightly, altered; and so the relations, proportions, values of each work of art towards the whole are reädjustable; and there is conformity between the old and the new.'

Which was, in 1923, a very significant move towards conceiving the Cultural Tradition as an organic development. . . . But the question of Tradition is a practical question, not one of theory, only. Tradition means a handing on, a giving over. The operation of Tradition, surely, should be the establishment of values: important basic matters that can be taken for granted, like table-manners and electric light, so that the work in hand may proceed untrammelled by the Past, but rather using its force spontaneously? Tradition in Art, for instance, should mean the installation, in the individual artist's equipment, of spiritual labour-saving devices: what Psychology calls Habits, on the 'physical' plane, Habitudes on the 'mental'. To quote Middleton Murry again:

'Unless society is an organic unity, in which the artist feels and knows himself spiritually secure, the undoubted concentration of his artistic faculty upon the created object is impossible. The necessary condition of great art is that the artist should be able to take elemental things for granted. . . . The artist to-day finds no spiritual authority which he instinctively acknowledges. . . . The artist who is conscious enough to be capable of great art is inevitably involved in the endeavour to discover or create the authority without which his activity as artist is either trivial or anarchic.'

And that endeavour is a waste of the highest energies, an unnecessary call upon the creative, the godlike faculties, which it should be the function of Tradition to conserve and use economically. Tradition must be an active force, not an abstract concept. Given a statement for the Nature of Tradition, in fact, it has to be asked: 'But what can you do with a Tradition like that?'

And what you can do with Mr. Eliot's Tradition, in his own, the literary field, is, apparently, to write a more and more self-conscious poetry, or culture-conscious poetry, or, at any rate, a poetry more painfully devised and intricately presented, though it may be, and in Mr. Eliot's own case is, a very fine poetry. You can learn up an inordinate amount of Literary History and obtrude your learning, partly as a defence mechanism, in culture-references, which are, at their subtler and doubtless higher level, what the 'How that reminds me of' order of remarks is in drawing-room conversation. As Tristan de Mussignac had it, partly misunderstanding John Keats, you can 'rift every ode with lore'. A single short poem of Marianne Moore's, for instance, invokes thirty other writers, and the author's notes, in consequence, are almost as extensive as her text. Tradition, in Literature, in Art generally, can, I believe, be restated as organic development, without the fallacies manifestly at work in these cases, or could be, if the conditions under which Art is produced and presented were not so unnatural as at present they are. But, for the moment, it is rather the development of the spoken language, from which Literature, by complicated processes, is derived, which presents us a pattern recognisably organic.

Or similar to that of Tradition in the Dance. . . . With which, after the sustained exercise of established disciplinary values, you can do a great many surprising, powerful and beautiful things with your body, in more perfect and subtle relationship, also, with other bodies: things that you never could do, without the cumulative force of Tradition behind you. The Ballet Style, the West's essential Art of Dance, is still capable of development, in ways that I hope to suggest. There will always be surprising, powerful and beautiful things that your body cannot yet do, nor your mind yet imagine, and you will always be trying, usually without your conscious knowledge, to reach them. But not by turning aside from that Muscular Memory embodied in the Classical Technique, to go whoring after some new— and easier (and payment is by results)—Romantic Technique of your own. . . . Perhaps the matter can be restated in this way: that there are certain qualities increasingly demanded from all the forms of human life, of which the forms of art are the clear pattern, and that Tradition— most substantially and therefore most valuably, as a pattern, in the Dance—is the force which establishes them.

Two such qualities, and perhaps the two most urgently and eternally demanded, being Impersonality and Precision. . . . The tendency has been, more and more patently, ever since the Renaissance, as I have suggested, to stress the importance of the individual, of Personality, against the impersonal community, and a great many of our present ills are certainly due to that tendency. Each of us, to-day, exists apart, each of us spinning more or less ecstatically on his own navel, closed up from the palpable reality of the physical environment: much more, then, from whatever single impersonal source of all life we may imagine, whether we call it Anima Mundi, the Racial Unconscious, Libido, the Universal Identity or, more simply, God. Hence, as any Freudian or Adlerian can tell you, all the various forms of Neurosis. . . . I have observed, elsewhere, that T. S. Eliot sought one kind of escape from the limitations of the self-contained little personal ego, in submitting to the spiritual and intellectual authority of the Church, and it was Impersonality he looked for in the Dance, when, at one moment, he turned to it. This, also, is the meaning of Mr. Eliot's attempts to state and live by Tradition, in the forms of art, and it is the most valuable part of his critical endeavour. The intention is—evaluating personal experience by referring your practice to 'the existing monuments' which form Mr. Eliot's 'ideal order among themselves'—to achieve Impersonality in the most intimate and personal things, to rule out idiosyncrasy and romantic extravagance and to have your eye left undisturbedly on the object.

From which 'undoubted concentration of the artistic faculty' the second quality of Precision. . . . In Literature, in the plastic arts, in Drama, in the Dance, in Art, altogether, and in Life, precise forms, the only durably beautiful forms, cannot be achieved but by complete reverence, in practice, for the endowments of the Past, for Tradition. Investigation of the matter of Isadora Duncan will show how and to what, in the Dance, comes a rejection of the traditional-precise, in favour of the anti-traditional glamorous-ineffable-vague. Here, let it be acknowledged, or reäcknowledged, that Ezra Pound's and T. S. Eliot's critical onslaughts on the glamorous-ineffable-vague in Literature, with the search for precise language-forms exemplified in their own creative practice, gave Poetry a substantial new spurt of life, when, in the work of their predecessors, in the Georgians, it looked dead for ever. The sad final truth is, however, that, with all its safeguards, with all its jealous striving for Impersonality and Precision, the poetry of Mr. Eliot, as of his followers and almost peers, remains very largely a private, an inaccessibly personal, and often an equivocal, a glamorous, an imprecise poetry. And the cause of this misfortune is that Poetry, now, is so cut off from its own roots that an active and sustained use of the force of Tradition has not been possible in the practice of these poets. There is no true Tradition which is not both cumulative and absolutely continuous, but, because the nineteenth century so vigorously falsified its own experience in Poetry, Mr. Eliot and Neoclassicism in general have found it necessary to reject the nineteenth and most of the eighteenth century, from their field of practical awareness, and to suppose that the spark will leap into them across a gap two centuries wide.

This, then, the dominant view of Tradition in Literature, has, in fact, found it possible to falsify itself completely, because it has not understood that, before the achievement of Precision and the surface realisation of Impersonality, comes the question of Power. And when Tradition as Power is operative, there is no discussion of the Meaning of Tradition, nor even much consciousness of it. Impersonality, for that matter, is never conscious of itself. Self-consciousness is self-distinction, is closed personality. A true and active Tradition is active and cumulative Power. It is necessary to be wary of the word Progress to-day, since the out-moded modish affectation is still to disallow the idea of Progress, very forcibly, as a mark of all that was most foul in the nineteenth century. But, in the Dance, at least, there is a movement which, if not Progress, is creative progression. There are the thirty-two fouettés, for instance, which nobody could do before Legnani, but which every true ballerina can do now, as though a new muscular faculty had been added to the human body.

'One day, when I was watching, I said to Matilde :"Try it like *this," and I put her in a certain position. "Tighten this muscle, and at every turn relax and contract it, making such and such a movement with the head." Up to that time she always fell about the seventh or eighth turn. The first time she tried my method she turned about a dozen times. Then she began working with me systematically, and soon acquired the thirty-two fouettés to perfection. A short time later she did Legnani's feat on the Mariinsky stage amid indescribable enthusiasm.'*

Such an event is unimaginable in Literary History. So is the visible handing on of the paraphernalia of Tradition from Christian Johanssen to Nicolas Legat. The only way the poet has, of adding to his stature, is by taking thought. Yet it was not so in primitive times. It need not be so in any true community. It is an assertion of Power. It is Tradition working in and through an active co-operation of artists in the creation of new forms, not abstract inanimate forms, but forms of behaviour.

And this, ultimately, is why the Classroom and the Theatre must be almost consubstantial, so that the operation of Tradition may be absolutely continuous. It is why a drifting company of dancers, without roots, must eventually—however brilliant the individual dancers and however finely organised—become infertile. It is why, in Literature, there will be no supremely great work again until poets can refresh and strengthen themselves, in direct and unbroken intercourse, at the springs of Living Speech, which rise up behind deliberate Poetry as Pedagogy does behind Choregraphy, in the Dance. Our poets would agree, doubtless. There is much talk, these days, of 'incorporating new speech-rhythms into the texture of our verse', and Mr. Eliot started that, too. But, when Living Speech is used in modern verse, as it is (particularly Chicago gangsterese), it is used in ironic, in culture-referent, in nostalgic ways. It is writing about, not in, Living Speech. Poetry is created in vital relation with the Tradition of Living Speech only when it is created among, for, with and, indeed, by the daily users of that speech. The poets most busy 'incorporating new speech-rhythms into the texture of our verse' are, unhappily, these days, the most 'highbrow', the most completely isolate poets.

The 'springs of Living Speech' must, as I say , 'rise up behind deliberate Poetry as Pedagogy does behind Choreography, in the Dance'. When this condition holds, Tradition will be untrammelled in its powerful operation. And it will not be talked about. It will be the implicit use of immanent powers. Evidently, this bears, for one thing, on the problem of the notation of ballets. Those who worry over this problem are wanting to make Tradition in Ballet the inanimate object of contemplation which it is conceived as in Poetry. They are wanting to establish an order of 'existing monuments'. They look with pleasure to the new possibility, offered by the Cinema, of inaugurating true Archives of the Dance, a vast array of museum-pieces. Naturally enough, from the foregoing, the thought that this must happen fills me, personally, with horror. It would certainly, be very pleasant to have complete and almost living images of Camargo, the Vestris, Taglioni, Pavlova, Nijinsky and now Markova, for all time. And I make no doubt that there is room for specially conceived Cinema Ballets (the possible form of which will suggest itself best to those who enjoy Walt Disney's work). But the wish to preserve choreographic forms as a kind of kinetic art-gallery and work on them as a basis must involve us in too much deliberate pastiche, too abstract a Frame of

Reference, too mental and self-conscious an approach to Choregraphy, developing into the situation described for Literature, with all its attendant nostalgias and methods of culture-reference.

The only system of notation needed, for Ballet to flourish, indeed, is that preserved in the nerves and muscles of dancers and teachers, co-operating actively and continuously: what I have called Muscular Memory. Some writers have already suspected that many of the accumulating ills of Poetry proceed gradually from the invention of printing, the comprehensive system of notation in Literature. They have clamoured for the restoration of an Oral Tradition. Rightly, as I think. . . . Poetry carried on as the great epics were, the ballads and the older minstrelsy (and as only funny stories are, now), changes its forms in their passage from person to person, so that when, at last, they come to be written down, they are a composite, a communal creation. Obviously, this notion does not please us to-day, for we look upon art as an intimately, even an aggressively, personal matter (like Religion since the Renaissance). The artist, above all men, must be allowed to spin ecstatically on his own navel. But, surely, in a healthy community, these mutations of chance, this diffusion of forms, can only enrich the central creative idea, together with the communal life as a whole? There is more to say about this, but let me annoy every right-thinking balletomaniac and amateur professor of the arts, for the moment, simply by saying that the true Tradition, for all creative activity, is most clearly and widely exemplified, at present, in the processes of preservation and ramification of the communal wealth of dirty stories, the Oral Tradition of Pornography.

The Russian School and the Meaning of Tradition

And in the Dance, at a fuller and richer level, less clearly, now, and less widely, but more substantially, giving us, so, a substantial pattern for human life as a whole. . . . One of the forestaters of Mr. Eliot's Tradition in matters intellectual and spiritual, T. E. Hulme, opposed to each other two fundamental views of Man, identifying them with Romanticism and Classicism, respectively: the one envisaging Man as 'an infinite reservoir of possibilities' (which might be shortened to an Ape on the Make) and the other as a sinful creature with a soul to save, such 'an extraordinarily fixed and limited animal' that 'it is only by tradition and organisation that anything decent can be got out of him'. Hulme himself, with Neoclassicism in general, endorsed the latter view, holding a brief for Original Sin and against Progress. In the Dance, however, these two views become one view.

For, watching a great dancer, it inevitably comes into your head to remember Hamlet and exclaim again on what a piece of work is Man, though Man, in his natural state, plainly, is a thoroughly unsatisfactory piece of work: in form, in moving, far from express and admirable, as a rule, and much less like an angel, in action, than a well-bred whippet is. The lines of even a fine human body are bad, outside a very small range of movements. And Ballet, fundamentally, is an attempt to defeat this fact, to reveal Man as, also, 'an infinite reservoir of possibilities', which, however, needs Tradition and Organisation, as the commoner kind of reservoir needs filters and drain-pipes. In Ballet, if I may quote myself again:

'*With the dancer, it is a struggle between a wastefully complex muscular system, designed for a limited range of animal acts and offices, and the economy, the simplicity, in line and mass, of the*

*postures and movements—the Physical Ideas—to which his body,
as a material of Art, aspires.'*

And the result is not a triumph of Mind over Matter, but
the emergence of non-cerebral Matter into such a condition of subtlety and sensibility that it can itself be called
Mind. So we ought to shift Hamlet's misplaced enthusiasm
and say what a piece of substantial thought and feeling was
Nijinsky. What a fresh and powerful flame of nervous
music. . . . And it was possible only through the Classical
Tradition.

That this Tradition should carry along, also, a weight of
artificiality and seemingly useless conventions is natural.
The danger is, in deciding too sharply what is useless and
to be rejected, that something essential may be rejected,
at the same time. To the temperamental enemies of Ballet,
and to those who clamour for Freedom, for the Natural, in
the Dance, it has to be pointed out that a basis of artificiality, of ground-conventions, is essential to all art-forms.
Artificiality provides for coherence in Style. A major
source of offence to many people, animated dolls, for instance, are one excellent occasion for the exercise of Style,
and the first ballet, after all, to effect a tragic Catharsis in
its own kind, or to be altogether satisfying as Drama, was
an animated-doll ballet, *Petrouchka*. The ballet skirt may be
discarded, often, but it remains, along with the extreme
turning-out of the legs and thighs, the conventional flut-
ters and mimic expressions and the formal display of the
Adagio, among the honourable attributes of that Art of
Dance which Europe has spent itself to evolve, prepared,
now, for application in countless ways, but not, by any
means, for supersession. Formalisation—of dress, not
least—will always be necessary. A woman on her points,

for instance, because of change in significant line and stress and action, ceases to be significantly a woman. She becomes an idealised and stylised creature of the Theatre and must be dressed accordingly. And all this Idealisation is part of the dancer's and the choregrapher's and the onlooker's struggle. It must be seen as essential to the system of tensions from which Ballet derives and in which it subsists.

There is also the balletomaniac, a creature of Tradition, to be explained away, but that is Society's job, not, as an apologist for Ballet, mine. This frequenter of all Ballet, this trailer-round after glamour, living in the vicarious glow of dancers, justifying himself by his knowledge of who can and who cannot do this or that act of virtuosity, by his never having missed a performance of Ballet since such and such a year and by his permission to address these and those dancers by their Christian names: this odd creature, with his coreless, amorphous, amœboid being, who can organise himself only by folding himself around the vigours and precise structures of an art in which he can take no active part. . . . The true balletomaniac is certainly an offence, whether he sits in the stalls, in a permanent boiled shirt, or in the gallery, in a perpetually changing fancy shirt, and whether he is a nasty old gentleman or simply an unhappy young one. But he impugns, as I say, Society, not Ballet. In Imperial Russia, Balletomania was by way of being a definite polite career, alternative to the Army and the Navy, or Diplomacy. Such and such an émigré, wishing to account for his social worth, will tell you that his father was a great general, a great statesman or, indifferently, a great balletomaniac. There were Les Dîners des Balletomanes, at The Cuba, in St. Petersburg, social occasions of the highest importance. Nowadays, in the vocation of Balletomania, there is more individual neurosis than collective neurosis (which is to say, snobbery). In other generations, under different social conditions, possibly Balletomania will be a form of religious fanaticism or, perhaps, of revolutionary horseplay. The balletomaniac has his uses in Society, particularly as a precise symptom of disease; but he is irrelevant to the structure of Ballet (for he can be conditioned to like any kind of ballets, equally), only showing, as elsewhere, the attraction of supreme vigour and delicate organisation for its opposites, as good Boxing or All-in Wrestling attracts one kind of well-bred hysterical woman, the celebrated sexual prowess of the negro gigolo another.

Similarly, to the rude noises of the very manly men, like Wyndham Lewis, with his 'Diaghilev's epicene circus', we have to say that we know all about it and are not really worried. Ballet itself is epicene, grant it. Art is. Major works of art, in any medium, are epicene. The Condition of Music is a Neutralisation. And this shows clearer, more vulnerably, in Ballet, because the elements, the artistic material, is human bodies. In Ballet, the human organism is not only producer and consumer, but the goods, also, and æsthetic goods, like the angels, have no sex. This does not mean that only the third and fourth sexes may dance: actually, the manly man and the womanly woman dance best (though the fact was momently hidden by Diaghilev, for more than one reason). Nor does it mean that the kind of nancy-boy who is disgusting in everyday life can be tolerable in Ballet. But it does mean that aggressive masculinity or aggressive femininity is as destructive of the essential stylistic conditions of Ballet as flaunted inversion is, if not more so. Hair on the chest is simply unnecessary, is superfluous hair. Appeal, of any kind, in fact, is out of place. Style—with Ripeness—is All.

It is in the understanding of this truth that Nicolas Legat still works his five to twelve hours a day, in his Fulham studios, for which I do not think I have honoured him to excess. We have lost the capacity for reverence. In the literary world, at least, it is an homage we reserve for one man, William Butler Yeats. One thing we might relearn from India is reverence for The Teacher, the guru. In Ballet, certainly, he is of more importance than even the Choregrapher, the poet, the creator, or even the Dancer. Nicolas Legat preserves and extends the Classical Tradition, in Fulham, with a pale-blue vestal watering-can and a priestly grand piano, on which he improvises. English misses come to this studio (but Toumanova comes, and Massine has come running for help on many a ticklish point) in order that the West's foot may be properly arched, the West's hip firmly tucked in and the West's below-the-waist strength and above-the-waist fluidity be joined by a supple back. Much stretching of legs along the bars; much beating of the feet to achieve the brisk entrechat, with the straight knee; much presentation of the whole body, with lightly profiled hands, in formal arabesques and attitudes; much weariness, aching, panting and sweat; no departure from the strict classical manner. . . . Do you cavil at such rigidity? A whole culture has spent itself to evolve the entire self-revelation of the Adagio and the concave (that is, the super-straight) leg of Alicia Markova. The classical discipline can be modified when something is evolved that includes—not merely surpasses—these phenomena.

I have heard it said, by a good many young dancers, that

Legat is not so good a teacher as he was, because, for instance, he does not correct enough. It may be true. It would be odd if it were not so. But it is, all the same, a rather naïve observation. I have been in other schools where there is so much shouting of criticism and correction that the atmosphere is like the atmosphere of a public swimming-bath, for echoes. These schools produce good and efficient dancers, quickly, which may be important for this modern world, but they will not produce great dancers. An occasional word from Legat, with his still miraculous eye for the muscle slightly out of place, does more if slower good than all this. The Dancer needs, for his fullness of development, a quiet ritualistic setting, where his muscles may become more and more sensitive and delicate in response, till they are swifter and keener and more clearly articulate than his mind: till his body is like the mind of a great musician or mathematician, with a plastic style that only the greatest painter and sculptor reach to.

But there is a box of camellias on the piano, sent by some admirer, some old Russian balletomaniac, probably, who remembers Nicolas Legat in the Imperial Mariinsky Theatre. The Maestro notices it, while he is playing, and chuckles. He takes out a camellia, at the close of the enchaînement, and puts it in his buttonhole. If I am in favour, he leans over and puts one in my buttonhole, too, and I feel very pleased about it.

III. The Sexual Idiom

I never saw Isadora Duncan dance. That, I believe, may
well be my best qualification for writing about her.
For it seems that nobody who did see her was able to
tell about her sanely. I know the music she interpreted.
There are hundreds of photographs and drawings of her
interpreting that music. Her autobiography is there, and
her many articles on the Art of the Dance, for anybody to
read. There are the many writings of those who saw and
knew her, varying in waftiness and hysteria, from those of
Mary Desti and Sewell Stokes to the brief obituary pane-
gyric of Max Eastman. Above all, there are the many new
schools of dancing which derived their forms and their
energy from Isadora and which are, for the present day,
much more important than she.

These I have watched and read, heard and seen, and I
have seen Nicolas Legat (who was asked, in 1905, to join
Isadora) frisk about with imaginary skirts, lift up swooning
arms and speak the word 'pornographique' most expres-
sively. Evidently, if I had seen Isadora Duncan dance, there
would have been no chance of critical sanity. With such a
woman, you must either be outraged, or laugh, or fall

cataclysmically in love; and find yourself in Jericho, anyway. I fancy I should have fallen in love. With such a woman and therefore with the art of such a woman. . . . It was all one. The art was the woman. It was the embellishment and justification of her extraordinary womanhood.

And the woman—which is to say, the little girl—was born under Aphrodite. She says, into the bargain:

'If people ask me when I began to dance I reply, "In my mother's womb, probably as a result of the oysters and champagne—the food of Aphrodite."'

She was born, too, beside the sea, and her 'first idea of movement, of the dance, certainly came from the rhythm of the waves'—from which Aphrodite rose. Her antecedents were just what they should have been: American Rationalism, of the plains and the skyscrapers, the America of Walt Whitman, entangled round a hot core of renegade Irish Catholicism. The family was poor. There were three brothers and sisters, Augustin, Elizabeth and Raymond. The mother was a grass widow. Conditions which make, altogether, for an oddly passionate family unity. . . . And the mother played Schubert and Chopin, and they all read romantic poetry.

Isadora danced, as we say, from the cradle. Growing up, there was local enthusiasm and misfortunes, provincial tournées, Augustin Daly, New York, and then the whole family betook itself to Europe, on a cattle-boat, to London, first, with Chelsea garrets and all the proper appurtenances of struggling art. Days spent in the British Museum, copying figures from the Grecian urns, from which Raymond Duncan eventually worked out a system of eight positions as seemingly fundamental as the five positions of Ballet. . . . Encounters, gradually, with the great: with Mrs. Patrick

Campbell, Ellen Terry, Sir Henry Irving. . . . A tour with Sir Frank Benson playing the first fairy in *A Midsummer Night's Dream,* for it 'seemed that theatre managers were unable to understand. . . .'

'In fact, at that time, it was difficult for me to understand why, when I had awakened a frenzy of enthusiasm and admiration in such men as Andrew Lang, Watts, Sir Edwin Arnold, Austin Dobson, Charles Hallé—in all the painters and poets whom I had met in London—the theatre managers remained unmoved, as if the message of my Art were too spiritual for their gross material-istic comprehension.'

Thence to Paris, to similar unremunerative or insufficiently remunerative frenzies of enthusiasm and admiration. . . . And Isadora, though fluttered by the great Rodin's sculp-turous advances, tried herself out, there, with remarkably elaborate deliberation, for so young a virgin, on two lovers, both of whom, however, were scared and fled.

Off to Germany, then, to Berlin, and to Vienna, with Loie Fuller; to Hungary, where the first more or less satisfactory lover was found, in a young actor, Romeo; and back to Germany, to Munich, to start the legend of 'die göttliche, heilige Isadora'; away to Florence, back to Berlin and its pseudo-Hellenism, away to Venice. . . . And then to Greece, the Glory that was Greece, the home of sea-born Aphrodite and the kin of Aphrodite, Apollo, Dionysus, greater than Apollo, and the haven of Isadora's most expansive visions and yearnings. . . . The Grecian ex-cursion is certainly the most fantastic episode in Isadora Duncan's fantastic life, and it is worth retracing, in some detail, before we come to more general non-biographical considerations. Raymond seems to have been the Hellenist of the family (of which Isadora's genius, of course, was the source of income), and he made the arrangements. From Brindisi to Santa Maura, first, paying homage, with suitable quotations from Byron, to Odysseus' Ithaca and the rock from which Sappho flung herself to drown; thence through the Ionian sea, the Ambracian gulf, Karvasaras, where Isadora and Raymond knelt down and kissed the soil, still declaiming Byron, to the great surprise of the natives. . . . There is not space for all the pagan raptures of the Clan Duncan. But Lord Byron continued to be the guiding genius of their Odyssey, until, by coach, paddle-boat and train, by way of the Acheloüs river, the ancient city of Stratos with its Temple of Zeus on the West hill, Agrinion, Missolonghi, Byron's heart and Shelley's, and Patras, they had come to the ultimate Athens. There they were joined by Augustin Duncan's wife and child, and there they decided to live for ever and build a temple.

They started by discarding the habiliments of Bohemia and putting on those of Ancient Hellas. Fitted with tunic, chlamys and peplum, with filleted hair and gnarled staves, they sought through Colonos, Phaleron and all the vales of Attica and finally lighted on Kopanos, miles from Athens, but a site on the level of the Acropolis, in a pilgrimage to the honeyed Hymettus. Land on Kopanos was immediately and expensively bought from the peasants: rocky land, with no growth but thistles. Raymond made out plans, after those of the Palace of Agamemnon. Red stone from Mount Pentelicus was brought, by long processions of carts, for many days. A Greek priest was asked to perform the elaborate ceremony of laying the corner-stone, with dancing and singing and the sacrifice of a black cock at sunset. A great feast was held, with barrels of raki for the peasants, the scheme of a kind of Pantisocracy drawn up,

which included a vegetarian diet, and the building under-
taken. And then, after a visit from the King, it was noticed,
for the first time, despite the rock and thistles, that there
was no water nearer than four kilometres. An Artesian well
was started, but the Clan Duncan spent more and more
time in Athens, on the Acropolis, in the Theatre of
Dionysus.

The phantasy's next phase was musical, not architectural.
In moonlight, in the Theatre of Dionysus, boys' voices
were heard singing in an antique mode. To revive the old
Greek chorus. . . . A large distribution of drachmas assured much competition, and soon, with the help of a
young and scholarly seminarist, a choir was formed and
taught to sing to the words of The Suppliants of Æschylus
—in the belief, or hope, encouraged by many students of
Byzantine music, 'that the hymns of Apollo, Aphrodite and
all the pagan gods had found their way through transformations into the Greek Church'. There was a pilgrimage to
Eleusis, passing by the Isle of Salamis, where Isadora's store
of culture-references was enlarged, to hold parts of Gilbert
Murray's translation of *The Persians* and 'a group of shadowy
initiates—Æschylus, Euripides, Sophocles, and Aristo-
phanes'. There was also a share in a revolutionary demonstration about the Greek stage language, a royal command
performance and some community singing. And then, at
the end of a whole year in Hellas, the Duncans were off,
with their seminarist and ten beautiful Greek boys in san-
dals and tunics. They took the boys to Vienna, Munich,
Berlin, with varied success, performing *The Suppliants*, with
Isadora as fifty Danaïdes and much academic applause. But
the voices began to break, the seminarist to lose his enthusiasm, the police to be worried about some of the boys'

activities. And the Greek chorus, quite soon, was taken down to Wertheimer's big department store, fitted out with ready-made knickerbockers and shipped off, back to Athens.

I urge a high admiration for the energy and consistency with which Isadora sustained the phantasy of that Grecian excursion (with the presence of the family, who must have been rather nice, though they were evident humbugs, to keep up the necessary semblance of a sense of humour). She was a whole woman, most whole, perhaps, in her grand-manner follies and vulgarities, and she responded wholly to her blood's images of Aphrodite and Apollo, Dionysus, Minerva, Zeus. The pictures of her, with arms straining aloft, at the Parthenon, are never altogether cheap, however ridiculous they may seem. Stupidly, perhaps, and certainly with a great deal of confusion, she was submitting herself with all the profundity of her womanhood, to a real if forgotten splendour. She was seeking contact, in the deep passivity of racial experience, with the energies that had produced, as well as some of the greatest art, the richest and most satisfying of all our mythologies. But Isadora Duncan was the complete eclectic. She had no intellectual control over her experience, to keep it, in a possible metaphor, from evaporating. And a new phantasy presented itself, as the old one came to a circumstantial end. Isadora studied Glück, read Kant (just as though an Isadora might have something to do with Pure Reason) and Nietzsche, who drew the diffuse and incoherent mass of Grecian images to the focus of the single myth of Dionysus; and then went off to Bayreuth, to replace the satin slipper with the transparent tunic, in Wagner's heavily languorous Venusberg.

The Sexual Idiom

It would be difficult to find two divinities more essentially remote from each other than the Hellenic Aphrodite and Wagner's sonorously lavish Teuton Venus; but the name, the cognate persons of Love Incarnate in Woman's Form, was enough for Isadora, and she shifted her allegiance with no great effort. Her own erotic state changed as easily. In Bayreuth, she was adored by Heinrich Thode, with a cerebral passion to which her response, as she records it, is illuminating.

'The rehearsal at Bayreuth began. With Thode I sat in the darkened theatre and listened to the first notes of the Prelude of Parsifal. The feeling of delight through all my nerves became so poignant that the slightest touch of his arm sent such thrills of ecstasy through me that I turned sick and faint, with the sweet, gnawing, painful pleasure. It revolved in my head like a thousand whirls of myriad lights. It throbbed in my throat with such joy that I wanted to cry out. Often I felt his slight hand pressed over my lips to silence the sighs and little groans that I could not control. It was as if every nerve in my body arrived at that climax of love which is generally limited to the instant; and hummed with such insistence that I hardly knew whether it was utter joy or horrible suffering. My state partook of both, and I longed to cry out with Amfortas, to shriek with Kundry.

'Each night Thode came to Phillip's Ruhe. He never caressed me as a lover, never sought even to undo my tunic or touch my breasts or my body in any way, although he knew that every pulse of it belonged only to him. Emotions I had not known to exist awoke under the gaze of his eyes. Sensations so ecstatic and terrible that I often felt the pleasure was killing me, and fainted away, to awaken again to the light of those wonderful eyes. He so completely possessed my soul that it seemed it was only possible to gaze into his eyes and long for death. For there was not, as in earthly

99

*love, any satisfaction or rest, but always this delirious thirst for a
point that I required.*

'*I completely lost my appetite for food, and even for sleep.
Only the music of* Parsifal *brought me to the point where I dis-
solved into tears and wept, and that seemed to give some relief
from this exquisite and terrible state of loving which I had
entered.*'

The obvious comment, I suppose, is that Heinrich
Thode's behaviour, in keeping the proudly sensual Isadora,
for so long, in that feverishly and pervertedly heady state of
being, was almost unbelievably naughty: excusable, if at all,
only on the ground that Thode was, at the time, working
on his St. Francis and, quite evidently, needing his inspira-
tion for Santa Clara. More interesting, though, is the fact
that Isadora could suffer this state, gladly, for so long, and
that she could still write it up with such evident relish,
twenty years after. Isadora Duncan was a powerful and rich
being, if ever any woman was, but her power and her richness were essentially passive. Her essential nature was rather
to draw in, to absorb and assimilate—a kind of passional as
well as intellectual Eclecticism—than to expand, to give
out abundantly, as her extravagance and her thoroughly
uncontrolled dancing seem to show. The catalogue of her
lovers is not, in itself, uninteresting. But the significant
thing is the infinite variety of her total response to them.
For each of her lovers, she changed colour; she changed
form, completely. She was altogether fluid and able to be
transformed by any powerful man's will, transformed
wholly. Yet she was choosing her submissions. Each submission was a manifestation of the passive female power.
She was absorbing and assimilating the rich wills of her
men.

The Sexual Idiom

At the same time, there is a curious unreality about all her accounts. I have spoken of phantasies. I should have spoken rather of the forms of one great polymorphous phantasy: which was Isadora Duncan's most substantial reality. Her nature never took form. It was as vast and changing and as finally unchangeable as the sea. It was a phantasy which Isadora sustained throughout her life, which endures in her legend and which she herself never understood at all. Even after the death of her children and after a run of loves which would have served to mature any half-dozen normal women, there is still, to the end, an extraordinarily adolescent flavour about Isadora's erotic nature and understanding. Her lovers, certainly, were never real men. From Romeo to Sergei Essenin, from Goddon Craig to the inexhaustible spring of wealth, to Lohengrin, and from Walter Rummel to the last stevedore, they were all visions and phantasies themselves and fuel to feed the one great phantasy. Isadora Duncan was a woman of amazingly rich and open erotic nature. She was also, very definitely, a sensationist. She was also an exemplarily glamorous mother. She was also an exhibitionist in the grand manner. In her schools, where the bodies of young girls were to be wrought to a beauty the world had not known, there was also something of Sappho and the Isle of Lesbos. But it is the phantasy which dominates. The phantasy embraces and assimilates all these things. They are facets, only of the phantasy.

And Isadora's life was Phantasy throughout. It never came to any true form at all, though Isadora was a whole being, and responded wholly, in each one of her phases. Her transformations were whole transformations. But the whole pattern of her life is as extravagant, as flamboyant, as lawless, as its substance, its single incidents. If it flowered, its flowers were of nothing more substantial than the stuff of methyl flames, wavering, disappearing in the light, evanescent in the haze through which Isadora looked out on the world and never able to achieve, or even to conceive, the peace, the stillness, into which life must subside when it will form into the round assurance of bloomed fruit. Evidently, Isadora Duncan was a beautiful woman, but even her own physical woman's beauty seems unformed, hazy, fluid: the kind of beauty that is frail in all its heavy lushness, changing from moment to moment and open, vulnerable, to every brief mood.

What has all this to do with the Dance, though? Evidently, a great deal. . . . Quite evidently in Isadora's own case and quite as much, if less evidently, with every form of the Dance. . . . Isadora's dancing is the restless physical movement of her phantasy. But a phantasy is not only a fluid, a formless thing, rejecting clarity. It is also a private thing. It is also an internal thing. As soon as it loses its private nature, by formulation and communication, and becomes externalised and takes form, it ceases to be a phantasy. It becomes a myth. And a myth is a verbal entity. The communication of phantasies, their translation into Myth, is the origin of Literature. The Dance can have nothing to do with phantasies. It can have nothing to do with anything private and internal. Nor can it have any honest commerce with verbal entities. And the Dance's end is always to be precise in its forms. Its desire is Clarity. Isadora Duncan was not concerned to dance, not concerned with any clarity of plastic forms. She was concerned with the Dance only as part of her primarily sexual phantasy.

She was concerned, also, as she thought, with Expression. She thought she was expressing herself, her fluid self, in the Heraclitean flux of restless half-forms. But the Dance cannot express a phantasy. Its first end is not Expression at all, or expression only of itself, of certain general qualities of style and of a passionate clarification. She thought she was recreating, for her self-expression, the forms of the Greek Dance. But forms of the Dance have force only for the community in which and by which they were evolved and created. They themselves become phantasy and formless to an age in which they need to be re-created, nostalgically, yearningly, from museum images. She thought, after reading Nietzsche, that her art was Dionysian. But the Dance of Dionysus, before and above everything else, was a free expression of the ecstasy of the whole community, not an exhibition, to the rest of the community, of one member's private ecstasy. Its forms are valid only as communal ritualia. In the rhythmical movements which Isadora Duncan executed in public, she was not even articulating, expressing, communicating a phantasy. A phantasy is not capable of communication, except by translation into myth and by relation with precise forms. She was only exhibiting signs of the ecstasy she felt in her private contemplation of the phantasy. Which, of course, excited the onlookers enormously. . . . They wanted to share the ecstasy itself.

Isadora's Art was, in effect, then, merely an art of sexual display, and I would stress the 'merely'. Isadora was not conscious of the fact. Nor, I suppose, were most of the spectators. She and they thought they were enjoying a spiritual experience. Perhaps they were, but it was only in the mass stimulation of private phantasies. There was no communication, or no communication in terms exact enough to be terms of art. Isadora thought she served all the gods, both ancient and modern: Apollo and Dionysus, the power-gods of European Royalty, the freedom-gods of America and the compassion-gods of Revolutionary Russia. In reality, she remained faithful to her stars. She served Aphrodite only. Her art was aphrodisiac.

But all art is aphrodisiac, surely? No, all art is anti-aphrodisiac. All art engages sexual impulses (if only by deliberately eliminating them). It may even be that art is greater or lesser art according, precisely, to the strength and range of sexual impulses that it engages. But its function, as art, is to neutralise, to release, its engagements. In a Freudian term, art is always Sublimation. The need of the artist is to bring some intolerable pressure of passional experience—which will always be experience sexually charged, if not itself primarily sexual, since the passional being is primarily sexual—to the condition that I tried to describe, after Walter Pater, as the Condition of Music. A configuration of sexually charged experience is brought to the condition in which it can be contemplated as pure form, and a Catharsis is effected, a purgation of precisely those impulses or passions most strenuously engaged. The apparent process is usually a substitution of symbols for the passional realities, hypnotic and magical symbols to which the passional charge can be transferred, leaving no loose unresolved emotion, and which can be contemplated as formalised outward entities.

This is the mechanism of dreams according, more or less, to Freud. It is also the mechanism by which myths are produced, out of the intolerable pressure of primitive man's passional experience, out of pure erotic Phantasy. Initiation, the adventure of virginity, becomes an adventure, a dark and difficult entry, to the jewelled cave, ablaze with light, the Trophonian cave, Aladdin's cave; and modern man will endorse the myth's compulsion, its relation to his own phantasy. This is art, which transforms a surplus of sexual impulses into æsthetic contemplation. The materials of art may, however, be used in a contrary way. Stories, novels, pseudo-myths, are written and published, in vast quantities, weekly, whose sole function is in the stimulation of jaded or repressed sexual impulses. There are pictures, sometimes very finely painted pictures, whose intention and effect is the stimulation of sexual impulses, where these are jaded or repressed. There is the music of Wagner and Scriabin. But that which excites, instead of transforming and releasing, is Pornography, not Art, according, precisely, to the extent of its capacity for excitattion. And it derives from feeble or stifled impulses, which need aggravation, instead of over-powerful impulses, which need redirection and release. This distinction between Art and Pornography is not an academic one; and it need not be stressed, I hope, that it is a distinction of which the censor, who bans James Joyce and encourages Ethel M. Dell, is not aware. Nor is it, of course, a distinction which disallows Pornography under all circumstances.

All this shows up more clearly in the Dance than elsewhere. I have already said something, in dealing with Tradition, about what I am calling the Sexual Idiom of Ballet. I pointed out, for instance, that a woman on her points, 'because of change in significant line and stress and action, ceases to be significantly a woman. She becomes an idealised and stylised creature of the Theatre.' And there is a kind of eternal virginity about her. She is inaccessible. She remains unravished. Or, in another light, another meta-phor, I said:

'*Major works of art, in any medium, are epicene. The Condi-tion of Music is a Neutralisation. And this shows clearer . . . in Ballet, because the elements, the artistic material, is human bodies. In Ballet, the human organism is not only producer and consumer, but the goods, also, and æsthetic goods, like the angels, have no sex. . . . Aggressive masculinity or aggressive femininity is as destructive of the essential stylistic conditions of Ballet as flaunted inversion is. . . . Appeal, of any kind, . . . is out of place. Style—with Ripeness—is All.*'

And Style, in human movement, is fundamentally that substitution of symbols for realities, the production of ideal forms out of the natural animal movements of the human body. To dance, to move flauntingly and with potent rhythmical compulsion, is to project a state of organic ex-citement which, by the nature of the organism, is neces-sarily sexual or sexually charged. Ballet, by the force and technique of Tradition, by its intricate channels of conven-tion, makes these states of organic excitement impersonal and transforms them, through its precise plastic forms, to states of artistic creation, the vicarious excitement of on-lookers to states of æsthetic contemplation. Ballet is su-premely the negation of Phantasy. Ballet is altogether con-crete, outward, precise and sheer.

But Isadora Duncan would have none of these precise forms, this transformation. She wished to retain, as valu-able in itself, the primary state of excitement, the personal ecstasy, and exhibit her state—communicating nothing but the excitation itself and perhaps something, vaguely, of its quality, its general tone—in movements which, she clam-oured, must be free, their only semblance of form proceed-

ing from the actual phase of her master phantasy. Look at
the countless drawings and photographs of her. . . . She
leaps along, knees thrusting upward in an agitation of the
loins, head either plunging down to knees or flung back in
taunting pride or turned in the glad terror of amorous
flight. In her more serious dances, her arms cease to float
caressingly but strain upward, trembling, in the infinity of
desire or are flung wide in the infinite welcome of the
matriarchal bosom, or are turned in, hands pressed over
breast in spiritual hurt. Or she glides onward, in a
tranced *lento cantabile*, in the plangent dream of fulfilment. And always, to end the exhibition, she strains herself
upward, again, at the heavens, the hazy Cosmos, the ether
streaming behind the stars. Or she falls in ecstatic swoon
to the floor and lies panting, in a flaccid lush supinity. None
of these movements is precise, sharp, clean, bright. There
is no control. There is no line. Everything is fluid, formless,
natural, free, without style, melting away, 'with its own
excitation, momently to mist'. The only dancing is the
dancing of a mist of loose drifting emotion. It was not an
exhibition of dancing. It was a display of Womanhood, of
the female principle as a hovering gaseous abstraction, as
Womanhood might be before it crystallised into functions
and social forms, seeking, swooning into, and yet resisting
forms.

And that is what Isadora was concerned with, not the
Dance. This is not authoritative. I did not see Isadora dance.
The material is there for anybody's reconsideration. This
case is an imaginative reconstruction, only, not dogmatic
statement. It is so overwhelmingly evident, though. With
the amazing physical and passional energy that she had, she
wished to create, not new forms for the Dance, but new

glamours for Womanhood; not finer art for the Theatre, but finer theatrical means for heightening the Female Mystery. She was not a dancer, but a sort of prophet. She thought she was both. She thought the Dancer was the greatest prophet. She speaks, always of the 'message' of her Art, and she speaks of her Art as 'spiritual'. She was concerned with the inward ineffable content. She was the glamorous matriarch, affirming, in herself, the glory of the primeval womb. She was, in fact, a bit of a feminist, a good deal of a suffragette. She wasted a lot of enthusiasm, for instance, on Emancipation, on 'the right of women to bear children outside marriage', and so on. All of which, evidently, has rather more to do with Mrs. Pankhurst and the Masculine Protest than with dancing (or, for that matter, with children). . . . But Isadora was of her generation, and her generation acclaimed her. She attracted to herself all the frustrations, yearnings, hysterias, of her generation. Many were found to acknowledge her prophetic nature. And that is where she ceases to be a great woman, an amazing femme fatale, a cause célèbre, a case, and becomes a nuisance. For, since her death, in the Dance, the Prophetic Nature has acquired an alarming popularity.

Isadora Duncan was—so—the female counterpart of David Herbert Lawrence, in Literature. Whether she was as great a person, it is difficult to say. Also, Lawrence often attempted art, as well as grim and cosmic Pornography. And it is certain that Isadora's work was inferior, as well as less durable. Lawrence used a medium which forced him to some precision. In Isadora's medium, of free movement, there was no range of such precise symbols as words to limit the glamorous-ineffable-vague. But the similarity between the two cases is close.

The Sexual Idiom

'*I spent long days and nights in the studio seeking that dance which might be the divine expression of the human spirit. . . . For hours I would stand quite still, my two hands folded between my breasts, covering the solar plexus. My mother often became alarmed to see me remain for such long intervals quite motionless as if in a trance—but I was seeking, and finally discovered, the central spring of all movement, the crater of motor power, the unity from which all diversions of movement are born, the mirror of vision for the creation of the dance—it was from this discovery that was born the theory on which I founded my school. The ballet school taught the pupils that this spring was found in the centre of the back at the base of the spine. From this axis, says the ballet master, arms, legs, and trunk must move freely, giving the result of an articulated puppet. This method produces an artificial mechanical movement not worthy of the soul. I, on the contrary, sought the source of the spiritual expression to flow into the channels of the body, filling it with vibrating light—the centrifugal force reflecting the spirit's vision. After many months, when I had learned to concentrate all my force to this one Centre, I found that thereafter when I listened to music the rays and vibrations of the music streamed to this one fount of light within me—there they reflected themselves in Spiritual Vision, not the brain's mirror, but the soul's, and from this vision I could express them in Dance.*'

This is Isadora (wherever she borrowed her terms) finding her way to the deep centre, the core, the dark source of all being, which Lawrence, also, demanded that we seek and live by. Both these modern prophets had the most unflinching belief in the positive power of the solar plexus and the unabateable flame in the womb. Each of them was concerned, above all, to assert the ideal ultimate of his own sexual principle, though both, sexually, were unhappy and forced to retreat into a phantasy: Isadora the

matriarch (would-be) and Lawrence the would-be patri-
arch, the Masculine Protest and the Œdipus Complex.
Both travelled over the world, endlessly seeking self-fulfil-
ment in alien images of the self-ideal. Both found their only
conceivable images in dead races, in museums: Isadora
among the monuments of the Glory that was Greece, and
Lawrence, with his wider field of reference, among the
Etruscans.

Both, in their questing, were anarchists, preachers of
chaos, of a return to the gaseous mindlessness of the
world's uncreated state. Both were anti-social. Both hated
the conditions which had produced them and sought, not
to change Civilisation's forms, but to escape into the
primeval womb of Civilisation. Yet both returned to their
place of birth. Lawrence came, at the end, to know that
the only place of his salvation was his place of birth. He
could not altogether desert the womb. And, after embrac-
ing every revolution and aristocratic counter-revolution
in the world of her time and of the old world, Isadora
yearned back to her origin and clamoured for the Dance
of America.

'*In one of his moments of prophetic love for America, Walt
Whitman said, "I hear America singing", and I can imagine the
mighty song . . . from the surge of the Pacific, over the plains, the
Voices rising of the vast Choral of children, youths, men and women singing Democracy. . . . I, too, had a Vision: the Vision of
America dancing a dance that would be the worthy expression of
the song. . . . It would have nothing to do with the sensual lilting
of the Jazz rhythm: . . . no rhythm from the waist down; but from
the solar plexus, the temporal home of the soul, upwards to the
Star-Spangled Banner of the sky which arches over that great*

stretch of land from the Pacific, over the Plains, over the Sierra Nevadas, over the Rocky Mountains to the Atlantic.

'*I pray you, Young American Composer, create the music for the dance that shall express the America of Walt Whitman, the America of Abraham Lincoln. . . . It is too mighty for the ears of most. But some day it will gush forth from the great stretches of earth, rain down from the vast sky spaces of stars, and the American will be expressed in some mighty music that will shape its chaos to Harmony.*

'*And this dance will have nothing in it either of the servile coquetry of the ballet or the sensual convulsion of the South African negro. It will be clean. I see America dancing, beautiful, strong, with one foot poised on the highest point of the Rockies, her two hands stretched out from the Atlantic to the Pacific, her fine head tossed to the sky, her forehead shining with a crown of a million stars.*

'*Why should our children bend the knee in that fastidious and servile dance, the Minuet, or twirl in the mazes of the false sentimentality of the Waltz? Rather let them come forth with great strides, leaps and bounds, with lifted foreheads and far-spread arms, dancing the language of our pioneers, the fortitude of our heroes, the justice, kindness, purity of our women, and through it all the inspired love and tenderness of our mothers.*

'*When the American children dance in this way, it will make of them Beautiful Beings worthy of the name of Democracy.*

'*That will be America dancing.*'

It will, indeed. It does seem, often, as though America has no antiseptic, at all, against the Bigger and Better, the Louder and Funnier. The important point is, though, that Isadora's Vision is paralleled with visions of New Britain, everywhere in Lawrence, till Mellors, Lady Chatterley's game-keeper lover, put the British Proletariat into scarlet tights, that would show the curve of leaping buttocks and the endless rippling of male muscle. But was it not, in both cases, personal regression to the womb? Salvation in the Derbyshire game-keeper, mastering the British Aristocracy, was the vision of David Herbert Lawrence, envisaging, from the womb, his own rebirth among his own people. And Isadora's was the Dance of America. America Dancing was the vision of Isadora Duncan Reborn. The two of them embodied, finally, the whole regressive lassitude of their generation.

They were types of the lassitude. Their generation found a focus in them, for all its own regressive phantasies, and yearned to them, with their greater fullness and courage and heaviness. Both attracted to themselves great numbers of hysterical people. Both lived in a haze of adulation. Both were hunted down, at first, as pornographers (which they were, but in my special sense, only). Both have subsequently become text-books of sexual behaviour, Mrs. Grundies of the days before the Deluge. The similarity extends into the minutest details of the legend. Lawrence is remembered as one who healed the commonplace. People have rhapsodised on his way of washing dishes. Isadora, according to Sewell Stokes, was lovely, perhaps most lovely, when she snored, and Mary Desti sees her getting drunk as a lovely slow flowering into heavenly beatitude and beneficence, expanding, 'like a flower, showering love on the whole world'.

Both, in fact, were more significant, finally, as persons than as artists. Both were archetypal persons, incarnating and thereby alleviating major dissatisfactions of their age. Lawrence is the more compelling. And the cause is almost wholly in his medium. I do not know—nobody will ever

know—whether Isadora Duncan may not have had as delicate sensibility, as great a spiritual nature, as D. H. Lawrence. Perhaps she had. But the significant thing is that the
use of words, symbols more or less exact, forced Lawrence
to clarification of his vision and phantasy and spiritual
perception. Whatever the value of his message, he did 'put
it across'. But what has a message to do with the Dance?
What has physical movement to do with expressing the
spiritual? If 'spiritual' means anything, it can only be used
of dancing which is as formally clear as Music must always
be, of bodily movement which has attained the final
clarity of spirit. Spiritual values are the gradual distillation
of a long process of Tradition. Isadora Duncan wanted to
manufacture them impromptu, out of brief ecstasies, trail-
ing clouds of loose emotional glory. She was striving to
recreate the Light that Never Was through a body that all
too substantially is.

In their negative significance, also, in the efficiency of
their anti-Traditionalism, Lawrence and Isadora are set
apart by the nature of their media. Lawrence rejected the
Intellect. Isadora rejected Ballet. And, in the two fields of
Literature and the Dance, the two things are cognate. Ballet, as pure technique and as pure stylistic employment of
technique, is very like what pure Intelligence is in Literature, what pure syntactical and metrical logic and form are
in the making of Literature. Lawrence, in rejecting Intellect, used Intellect. He denounced pure Intelligence, re-
nounced its possibilities for evil, in the most admirable employment and enjoyment of pure Intelligence. Finally, he
did great service to Intellect, enriching it, and so to Literature, as a whole and with all it touches. Isadora could use
no such means. She denounced Ballet, verbally, and danced

H   *113*

her own way. If she had mastered Ballet, as Lawrence mastered pure Intelligence, she could have enriched it and done service to the Dance as a whole. Merely rejecting Ballet, she remains irrelevant to the Dance, except in negative senses.

But perhaps we should look more closely at Isadora's relations with Ballet. The actual detail of Isadora's life has not been retraced beyond the return from the Grecian excursion to Bayreuth. Apart from the first Russian excursion, the direct confronting of Ballet, it is not necessary to retrace it any further. On the one hand, it is fairly familiar: the various lovers, the death of the children, the pitiful long mother-lover relation with the adolescent hooligan and rare poet, Sergei Essenin, the defection and final timely-tragic true femme-fatale death with her dancing shawl. On the other hand, it is irrelevant. In 1905, when she first went to Russia, Isadora Duncan was as nearly formed as she ever would be: which is to say, she was entered into the thick of her phantasy. And her art did not change, afterwards, so far as one can see. She relinquished it and returned to it, only, grew fat and grew thin, abandoned to it one new grief or joy and another and all the final lassitude. And she tried, continually, to form great schools, which never took the form she wanted them to. Contact with Isadora seemed to be enough to set her pupils off, having discovered their solar plexus, to vaunt their own prophetic natures and spiritual missions. And that is all. But the direct confronting of Ballet is important, to an Apology for Dancing. Isadora Duncan's objections to Ballet are pattern-objections for nearly all the modern world. This whole chapter should be read as a general defence of the Dance against the 'spiritual' dancers, the inward dancers, the free, the natural, the prophetic and the æsthetic dancers, the personal phantasists and exhibitionists. We can look at Isadora's protest against Ballet, and then we can come, casually enough, to those mushroom forms of the Dance which were fertilised by her or in any of many ways reflect her significance.

The arrival in St. Petersburg was well timed. On January 5th, 1905, Nicolas II, cowering in the Winter Palace, permitted his guard to shoot down a mass of workers who had gathered without weapons, in the square below, to petition His Imperial Majesty for bread. Isadora Duncan arrived at dawn the following day, and was greeted by a long procession of coffin-bearers, up so early to bury their comrades before the disaffected city was awake. Isadora wept, in the black Russian dawn. If she had not seen it, she says, all her life would have been different. There, before this seemingly endless procession, this tragedy, she vowed herself and her art to the service of the people and the down-trodden. Ah, how small and useless now seemed all her personal loves and sufferings! How useless even her art, unless it could help this. . . . So Isadora Duncan drove on to her palatial suite at the Europa and cried herself to sleep. Soon her room was filled with flowers. Two nights later, she appeared before the élite of St. Petersburg, in the Salle des Nobles, and was acclaimed by the Grand Duke Michel. Kchessinskaya called on her, to welcome her, on behalf of the Russian Imperial Ballet, and then Pavlova. Isadora was ravished by the artistry of these two heavenly beings, creatures of the Classical Tradition, the Dancer at his highest pure glamour. Then Pavlova took her to supper, after *Giselle*, with Bakst, Benois, Diaghilev and all the elect spirits of the Russian Intelligentsia. And Isadora (forgetting everything but her line of talk) proceeded to inveigh against Ballet.

She wanted Nature. She wanted the surge and lapping of the waves. She wanted the sapling trees, swaying in the breeze. She wanted to express—to be—these. She believed that the dawn and the sunset and the infinite wastes of the stars were lovelier, more rich in significance, than the choregraphic forms of Ballet. And so they are. In themselves they are more beautiful and môre richly significant—at any rate, more impressive—than anything to be seen in a theatre. But that is hardly the point. To strive to re-create them, in human movement, in the Theatre, is not greatly different from wanting to recreate oak panelling in glazed wall-paper, silk hats in ash-trays or votive candles in the glowing of electric-light bulbs. The beauty of any natural happening or natural thing is its identity, its particularity, its unique and inimitable quality. And in its native context. . . . We don't want a classical Adagio on the high hill. We don't want the movement of lapping waves in the Theatre. In the Theatre, the theatrical—and only the theatrical—is natural. If you wish to reject the theatrical, then you must reject the Theatre. That is what Isadora did not understand. It is what the innumerable schools of free, soulful, natural and prophetic dancing do not understand. It is also, I am afraid, what a good many contemporary choreographers, within Ballet, do not understand. They want to run everything into a formless whole. They want to run together the natural glamours of the Open Air (the poetical glamour of situation) and the arti-

Plate 4. Tatiana Riabouchinska in *Les Cent Baisers* (Nijinska). *Howard Coster Photograph.*

ficial glamours of the Theatre and make themselves one comprehensive Fairyland.

So, while enjoying in the highest degree the glamours of the Theatre, Isadora Duncan was able to turn out this line of talk. She was able to say that

'*The school of the ballet to-day, vainly striving against the natural laws of gravitation or the natural will of the individual, and working in discord in its form and movement with the form and movement of nature, produces a sterile movement which gives no birth to future movements, but dies as it is made.*

'*The expression of the modern school of ballet, wherein each action is an end, and no movement, pose or rhythm is successive or can be made to evolve succeeding action, is an expression of degeneration, of living death. All the movements of our modern ballet school are sterile movements because they are unnatural: their purpose is to create the delusion that the law of gravitation does not exist for them.*'

And so on. . . . And finally this . . .

'*To those who nevertheless still enjoy the movements, for historical or choreographic or whatever other reasons, to those I answer: They see no farther than the skirts and tricots. But look— under the skirts, under the tricots are dancing deformed muscles. Look still farther—underneath the muscles are deformed bones. A deformed skeleton is dancing before you. This deformation through incorrect dress and incorrect movement is the result of the training necessary to the ballet.*

'*The ballet condemns itself by enforcing the deformation of the beautiful woman's body! No historical, no choreographic reasons can prevail against that!*

'*It is the mission of all art to express the highest and most beautiful ideals of man. What ideals does the ballet express?*

'*No, the dance was once the most noble of all arts; and it shall be again. From the great depths to which it has fallen, it shall be raised. The dancer of the future shall attain so great a height that all other arts shall be helped thereby.*

'*To express what is the most moral, healthful and beautiful in art—this is the mission of the dancer and to this I dedicate my life.*'

When, in fact, they were not merely temperamental, Isadora's objections to Ballet were moral, not æsthetic. At her most serious (getting out of her phantasy), she was concerned with what is humane, what ought to be, what improves and uplifts, in the most obvious senses; and, if you have moralistic feelings first, whether particularly, about dancing, or generally, about living, then you must, ultimately, reject Ballet and follow on from Isadora. If you are concerned, however, with beauty and sheerness and the subduing power of movement that is superhuman enough to be slightly terrifying, then Ballet will seem to you the only dancing. Supposing Isadora—on 'deformation' —to be right in more than an infinitesimal degree (which, of course, she is not), it will seem to you proper that human bodies should sweat and ache, in the Classroom, and even become, for ordinary human purposes, constricted, reduced, perhaps, even ugly, so long as movement in the Theatre is more beautiful, sheer and compulsive. Reverting, again, to Tradition. . . . A definitely 'immoral' aspect is heightened in all art—in all life, for that matter—by the strong operation of Tradition. Tradition is something, always, of its own nature, to be struggled against. That is a large part of its function. The value of Tradition is fundamentally in the rich and fruitful conflicts and tensions set up between itself and the free human being. That is why continuous Religious Tradition, for instance, is spiritually necessary. And when either side yields or is violated, life becomes very poor and weak. By a violation of Tradition, we get Hollywood ethics and the welter of nasty Nonconformist sects. On the other hand, when the free individual life lets Tradition drain off all its energies, we get the hideous spectacle presented, almost unanimously, by the older generation in polite society. We get the incredible symbolic figure—it still exists, though!—of the withered old lady, with her scrutinising lorgnette. In Religion, we get a self-contained and inwardly sufficient churchy pietism which must certainly be as distasteful to God as it is to the unwithered creature. We get the Royal Academy. We get the verse of Mr Alfred Noyes. And these things, also, have their equivalents in the Dance.

But, even in purely physical terms, there is no strong beauty without strong tensions and conflicts. The leaping of a powerful animal is beautiful, but it is a beauty which soon reduces, when repeatedly presented, in different sets of conditions, to a commonplace. Its trajectory, for instance, is not much different from that of an alighting bird, a javelin or a cannon-ball. I think the loveliest single movement I ever saw—certainly the most 'unnatural', certainly terrible, certainly immoral—was that of a chained and ravenous animal. The chain being equated, I suppose, with Tradition. . . . On a very hot day, in the Schwarzwald, it was a lean and exasperated Great Dane, sheltering and sweltering in the barn-door of an inn, with its unusually long chain coiled by it. As two of us, tired and thirsty, came up to the inn (we had not seen the dog), it came out at us with a terrific howl, four or five yards out, two or three yards up, was caught and swung round in mid-air, at the length of its chain, and dragged back, by the tremendous recoil of its own power, with an amazing luscious planetary curve, crashing and shrieking against the barn-wall, making the whole building and the baked earth shud-der. No doubt, it was painful for the dog. It was also frightening for two human beings. But the pain and the fright did not last long. The moment's grip and rip of terrible beauty is indestructible.

Or is that only 'the curious local callousness of the artist'? Am I, in any case, taking too much trouble over Isadora? Was she not just a rather silly, rather vulgar, rather adorable woman, possessed of enormous energy? She is dead and done with. Let her rest. And so on. . . . But Isadora Duncan's importance for the present situation in the Dance cannot be exaggerated. It is not so much her direct influence, though the young Michel Fokine was given a tremendous initial impetus by her theories. It is rather that the same vicious demands of the age which brought her to the surface are also dominating Ballet, in-dependently. Ballet people, when they speak of her now, and of her successors, laugh at her and at them, heartily enough. But it remains fact that, for the most part, they themselves are demanding, from the Dance, just the same kinds—and sometimes, even, inferior kinds—of extrinsic and illegitimate satisfactions. Pure Style is at a discount, everywhere, in Ballet no less than in the innumerable kinds of Free Dancing. But the analysis of this situation be-longs to my last chapter, after a full vindication of my de-mand for Pure Style, unhelped by literary, moralistic or any other 'significances'. In the meantime, the schools of Free Dancing themselves are numerous enough and danger-ous enough. Every small-town teacher of dancing has her own particular brand of Freedom. And I believe that there are even more small-town teachers of dancing in America than in this country.

America, certainly, produced Ted Shawn, and, if you do still think that Ballet is cabin'd, cribb'd, confin'd and bound up with dead conventions, or suspect that Free Dancing may be either dancing or free; if you believe that Sturm und Drang is nobler than Moonlight and Muslin, or can argue that self-expression is different from exhibitionism; if, in fact, you would assert the claims of the Soul . . . then you should not miss the earliest opportunity that presents itself of watching this gentleman dance. Ted Shawn and his Ensemble of Men Dancers, done up in jock straps and shaven chests, almost fulfil, I should imagine, Isadora's vision of America Dancing. It is true that these limber lads, when they came to London, did not impress the Great British as they have impressed the Great American Public, so that to be heartily rude about them is unnecessary, as well as not cricket. But what our surprisingly sceptical critics did not well understand is that the perspiration of these young huskies is the ultimate essence of all Freedom in the Dance. If you want precision, speed and beautiful line—which is to say, if you will have dancing—then you must get it through all the rigours of the classical Ballet technique. Reject these, in favour of no matter what Romanticism, and, finally you will get Mr. Shawn, standing up and lying down, suffering, agonising inwardly, sweating, with cumulative profusion, for twenty minutes or so, to communicate, through his eyes and hair, the intestinal passion of a spurious John Brown in the face of an altogether non-existent or at least invisible Glory. Even within the apparent confines of Ballet, sweat down a monster like *Union Pacific*, and you will get something like Mr. Shawn's

March of the Proletariat, repeated later, with the addition of hats and an impression of clothes, as *Cutting the Sugar Cane*.

That dancing is no concern of the Ted Shawns of this world is shown clearest, perhaps, in the one important Ballet movement these dancers have adopted: a leaping circle of grands jetés—in which, however, the arms, pressed romantically back, behind the face (which they should frame), would break the heart of the most indifferent sculptor, let alone any Master of Ballet. And this, I suppose, is what all criticism of Free Dancers reduces to: that they do not dance. But let me not be thought to be blind to admirable effort. I have the greatest respect for the work of Margaret Morris, for instance, though she derives from Isadora more directly than any other school. Her remedial work, her work in athletic training, is, some of it, excellent. And I should be happy to see her courses substituted in public elementary schools, for the physical jerks—all too literally, jerks—of the present Government syllabuses. More than that. . . . Isadora Duncan was partly right in her argument that the Ballet training has a tendency to deform, at least, the bodies of children. A too early start in Ballet is vicious, in the case of all but the strongest children. Yet, if we are to have great dancers, there must be some training from the earliest years. And, if a national scheme were worked out, incorporating a good deal of Margaret Morris's work, there would, at the school-leaving age, be such a wealth of material for the true schools of the Dance as has never been dreamt of. Even Dalcroze Eurhythmics has its pedagogic justification. Only, these kinds of work, in practice, are useless for the Theatre.

And the work of Kurt Jooss—to some extent, also, that of the Central Europeans proper—escapes most of my

The Sexual Idiom

criticisms of Free Dancing. The Jooss Dancers are fundamentally concerned to evolve a technique for the Theatre,
not to exhibit themselves. Though there is not the cumulative force of centuries of Tradition, yet there is, here,
something of the impersonality of Ballet itself. The basic
argument against Kurt Jooss is, simply, that he has not made
up his mind whether it is Drama or the Dance that he is
concerned with. And that is an argument against most
specifically modern work in the World of Ballet, too. But
this is matter for the two last chapters.

A certain Impersonality—which means, in essence,
Responsibility—must also be allowed to such as La Argentina (Antonia Mercé), though they dance alone and are
celebrated, primarily, as unique theatrical personalities.
Dancers of markedly national character cannot be accused
of exhibitionism. However individual their technique, they
have, behind them, a Tradition older than that of true Ballet, which preserves their work from the indulgence of
private Phantasy. Argentina is quite spurious, in some
senses. The work she arranges to the music of Granados,
Albeñiz, de Falla (themselves rather spurious composers),
is not nearly what it pretends to be. But she has, I think, a
finer sense of the Theatre than any other dancer I have
seen. Her personality has been worth all that miraculously
careful stage-management. And her tricks cannot cover
over that impressive strangeness of the forms of the Spanish Dance, which consists in an intricate fusion of Eastern
and Western characteristics: the incoiling castañet-hyp-
notic incantatory structure of the Eastern Dance overlaid,
as it seems, with the flaunting outwardness of the West,
of the Bases of Ballet, with the two interplaying as intimately as the elements of a split personality. Still, failing a

123

real Flamenco on his native heath, I prefer my Spanish entirely Westernised and stylised, in Ballet, where it entered in Petipa's hey-day and where, more recently, it has found a new importance as the evident basis of Massine's peculiar heroic manner.

But then the whole simple truth about Free Dancing, is that there can be no such thing as Free Dancing. The human body is one mass of resistances, which are only partially broken down by a life's devotion to sustained principles of muscular technique. The Dancer must always be concerned, supremely, with muscle, not soul, not expression, not literary significance. Let me repeat the most fundamental grounds of my position.

'Man, in his natural state, plainly, is a thoroughly unsatisfactory piece of work: in form, in moving, far from express and admirable, as a rule, and much less like an angel, in action, than a well-bred whippet is. . . . And Ballet, fundamentally, is an attempt to defeat this fact, to reveal Man as, also, 'an infinite reservoir of possibilities', which, however, needs Tradition and Organisation, as the commoner kind of reservoir needs filters and drain-pipes. . . .It is a struggle between a wastefully complex muscular system, designed for a limited range of animal acts and offices, and the economy, the simplicity, in line and mass, of the postures and movements—the Physical Ideas—to which his body, as a material of Art, aspires. And the result is not a triumph of Mind over Matter, but the emergence of non-cerebral Matter into such a condition of subtlety and sensibility that it can itself be called Mind.'

For all Art, all Creation, is the end of a powerful and sustained love-pact between the Artist and his Material: his words, his musical tones, his pigments. There is courtship, long and difficult and delicate wooing, and the final-seeming creative act of love, which is never final. It shows clearest, perhaps, in Sculpture. The sculptor has to know every grain, every fibre, every substantial principle—the textures, the hot and cold, the humidities, the masses, the qualities of biting back on the chisel: all the resistances and all the potentialities—of the single block of wood or stone, before he can be fully ready and fit for the fruitful act of loving rape which satisfies himself and fulfils the material. It is the pattern of sexual love. It is the pattern of religious experience, where the soul is possessed and enjoyed and fulfilled by God.

The Dancer is hermaphrodite, in this. He commits rape and begets lovely forms in his own body, with continual increase of power. His material, the field of his creative experience, is his own muscular and nervous being. And his fulfilment is in the externalised joy of movement, the release, the building up of inherent tensions into a powerful system of release. This is the only true freedom. It is the kind of joy and freedom we call dancing. Not the joy of an inward, an unprojected ecstasy, which can only be communicated through erotic empathy and sympathy between the Dancer and the onlooker. . . . This is not Freedom. It may be a good kind of licence, but Freedom is a more difficult thing. It has to be achieved, as the end-product of a long and usually painful process.

And now, before we come to tackle the contemporary situation and make some critical forecast for the future, I have to justify the difficult achievement of that freedom. No process justifies itself. Music, Plastic, Poetry, are acknowledged to be, in one way or another, 'significant' to human life. They express and reveal. They are necessary and instructive to life. What I said of the Dance, generally, in my opening chapter, justifies the Dance only in literary terms, as a pattern. Since then, I have been chiefly engaged in saying what the Dance is not, in cutting it loose from accidental confusion with the functions of the other arts, from expressive functions, in particular. Divorced from Music, Plastic, Poetry and even from the Theatre, what, then (we have to ask), is the 'significance' of physical movement, in its own right? What 'values' has it, when, as in the Dance, it serves no useful, no utilitarian purpose, when, that is to say, it is its own end-product? These questions have to be answered. We need a Philosophy of Ballet. Otherwise, the Dance must still seem a futile matter, however pleasant, and worth the waste of no serious person's time and pains. But a Philosophy of Ballet? Yes, a Philosophy of Ballet. . . . Any serious justification must be metaphysical. The whole of life holds together, in a metaphysical way. But the title shouldn't be found inhibiting. There will not be very much more Philosophy, properly, than in the other chapters. In the orthodox sense, it will be a chapter against Philosophy.

IV. A Philosophy of Ballet

A. The Flesh Made Word

The general approach of Æsthetics and Critical Theory has always been through Poetry to the other arts. This, I suppose, might be called normal. Criticism uses the materials of Poetry, and the other arts have few conceptual elements able to be justly verbalised. But the disadvantages of this approach, the necessity of error in the procedure, are never escaped. The hard-boiled Nominalism of Dr. I. A. Richards has all the appearances of casting floods of light on Poetry. His remarkable impotence in the face of Music suggests the illusory nature of those appearances. Constant Lambert's survey of contemporary music (which I shall be quoting later) was a valuable, as well as a brilliant, book. It would have been an absurdity in any age when composers were not themselves working from literary premises. And the effect of verbal theories on the visual arts—despite a vigorous verbal rejection of the literary—is such that Lessing would need an infinitely subtler mind to make out his case to-day.

The main source of confusions seems to be one that Dr. Richards, at least, might have been expected rather to examine than to exploit. It lies, I believe, somewhere in or around the word 'abstract'. The fact that we commonly use words for communication has led us to suppose a closer essential nexus between word and attitude than between musical phrase or pictorial image and attitude; and this despite the acknowledged gestural origins of speech, the solving of the most involved problems—in mathematics, in chess—without verbal help, the fact that some of the most efficient minds (T. E. Hulme, for instance) have been almost pure visualists, and the flagrant ability of a vast majority of the human race to dispense with words except in their purely denotative capacity. It is only, indeed, because of a welter of daily accidents, casual associations, that words have come to seem more 'opaque', more 'three-dimensional', more solid and therefore more exact, than other counters: just as it is the verbal exigencies of spatial metaphor, together with Civilisation's over-development of sight at the expense of hearing, that has made contrast of colour and interplay of line more 'concrete' than tone volume and pitch-rhythm relations. If 'abstract' equals 'remote from sensual experience', then words—precisely because of their accidental richness of association—are effectively more abstract in artistic or in any deliberate and original manipulation, and pigments no less abstract, than the materials of Music. And any attempt to proceed to critical statement on a contrary assumption is assured, beforehand, of failure. The sad truth is that all modern art-materials have become so unreckonably abstract and operate so tortuously that introspection (a metaphorical term for a vast range of finely graded psychical events) is probably still the least bewildering approach we have to art—by way of those materials.

I have already stated the purpose of this chapter. It intends a metaphysical justification of Ballet. But it is also by way of being notes, more generally, for a Human Approach to Art. The phrase is suspect, naturally. Human approaches to art have previously meant denuding the arts of their difficult human significance and offering them to The Man in the Street as a quite superfluous endorsement of his daily attitudes. What is meant here, however, is an approach to other arts—or to Art—by way of those two arts, of the Dance and of Song, in which human organs, in which the human organism is, originally, the total material, in which the total artistic process (continuous, therefore) takes place within the organism; in which, in fact, the human being is not only producer and consumer, but the goods, also. That is to say, it is an approach to the Abstract by way of the Concrete, for the 'concrete' elements of other arts, now, are notation, and only that. As is proper to notes, no sustained argument, or the ghost of one only, inheres. I am concerned with the other arts, here, only in so far as they bear on the Dance. Apart from that, any value there may be will reside in incidental and haphazard suggestions. And the shape of an argument—cyclic—will be provided by the implication that this Human Approach is more apt to the West than to the East: wheels within these wheels being supplied by a belief that the kind of verbal approach instanced represents—metaphysically, if not historically—an Easternising.

But, first, it is necessary to put away the idea Communication, in favour of the idea Articulation. Communication presupposes Articulation. Historically—and genetically, for the individual—there are modes of articulation before there are modes of communication. And a main difference between the two processes is that any act of communication implies intention, purposive if not strictly conscious, while no mode of articulation is necessarily bound up with other than spontaneous organic impulses. So Articulation may be defined, for present purposes, as such dispositions of human energies as imply no preparation for action (appropriate to situations in which Articulation takes place), but constitute in themselves the final translation (into terms of nervous and muscular effort, of whatever kind) of implied complexes of experience. It is not necessary, for the moment, to be more precise. But it may be helpful, to students of Dr. Richards' work, to observe that, in this view, the Riccardian 'attitude' may be considered as occurring 'between' a given complex of experience and its articulation, in the same way as, in common psychological usage, Emotion occurs 'between' Cognition and Conation, seeing and acting.

And, from this, we can go on to show that Man has two fundamental modes of articulation. One of these is the vocal mode. It comprises such noises as sighs, groans, moans, sobs and a variety of amorous and other cries which it would be even more embarrassing to list. Some of these articulations (because of their perceptible correspondence with quite simple emotional states) indicate their root complexes of experience with fair precision and so acquire a communicative function. When a man, in the situation describable, broadly, as hammering a nail into a wall, ejaculates—'Ow!'—it is pretty obvious what has happened. And, if someone else is present, the articulation does communicate, more or less exactly, what he is feeling. But 'Ow!' and its like are not essentially communicative. Communication is not their first function. Rather, they are nervous and muscular resolutions of complexes of experience—end-products, as poems are—permitting, as we say, a feeling of relief or peace. 'That's right, darling. You go on and have a good cry. It'll do you good.' And so on. . . . This mode of articulation has been fairly adequately recognised, however, and (apart from the fact that sobs and groans are not yet perceived, as a notable contemporary might say, to be objects worthy of serious critical attention) there is no need to spread oneself about it, here. But the significance of a second mode—that of Gesture—has, when considered at all, by anthropologists and others, been utterly baulked and smothered, and any attempt to reconsider it is good.

There are a great many spontaneous local gestures, of the hands, of the facial muscles, which appear to have some original articulatory force and which certainly come to have communicative force. But these link up closely with the functions of speech and are not able to be studied, in any pure state, in a self-conscious society, though anybody who has observed a thoroughly tired housewife pass her hands strongly and very slowly over her face (for that matter, any thoughtful actor or producer) will not find the belief fantastical that they can have more than a purely expressive value.[2] What has more importance, however, is

---

[2] One important testimony, here, is that of the Behaviourists (and of some other psychologists) who insist that Emotion is—not 'is expressed by'—distortion of physical moment. Behaviourism is falsified, as a whole, by the fact that, like the most idealistic and the most introspective psychologies, it attempts to draw all Behaviour into the embrace of a very limited range of formulæ. But it represents valuable tendencies, not only by its insistence on particulars like this, but by its resolute objectivity, its concentration on the pure phenomenon, the minute particulars, in a world which is otherwise divided between intellectual proliferation and navel-gazing.

that there are certainly obviously non-communicative gestures which involve, moreover, the totality of the organism; a configuration, in stress and relaxation, of every muscle, and which probably, therefore, involve, also, complexes of experience forcibly and significantly operative in
the whole of the nervous system. Four such gestures are
clearly distinguishable and may be called cardinal: that of
tense maximal erectness, that of kneeling (unpremeditated,
not as a deliberate sign of devotion or submission), that of
bracing the body hard against the face of some great object
(rock, tree-trunk, wall) and that of such a form of complete prostration as implies no direct or primitive-sur-
vival attempt either to hide from danger, natural or super-
natural, or to express subjection.

Here, again, some embarrassment must be felt in treat-
ing of these matters in bald prose: testimony, in itself, I
think, to the truth of what follows. But the importance of
these four gestures, performed spontaneously, is not well
ignored. And so, especially since there is no other available
reference, perhaps I may be forgiven for reprinting, in full,
a piece of writing done, in lush intuitive heat, about three
years ago.

'*There are these Great Gestures.*

'*First, there is that Gesture in which a man directs his whole
body upward. The muscles of his stomach press down, and his ribs
spread wide to take all the air that pours in at the nostrils. His
breast lifts high, the head pressed back, and his right arm
thrusts up, into the air, rigid, the fist clenched hard, taking the
whole posture's main stress, perhaps trembling with unsatisfied
effort, eyes are calm and grave, and brows level, the forehead
uncreased.*

'*In the second place, there is that Gesture which slowly bows a* man's head, his eyes a little over-solemn, over-tender, perhaps, often closed, his shoulders drooping forward and his arms limp, though the hands may be lightly clenched. Then, quickly, with a yielding of the whole frame and probably a second of unconsciousness, he sinks down to his knees. Tension is restored. His eyes are untroubled, his limbs wholly possessed. He raises his head, but does not press it back. His face is turned upward, eyes like his who makes the First Gesture, but the mouth is looser, the lips parted a little, sensitive to the air.

'The Third Great Gesture is a bracing of the body against some broad strong thing, the trunk of an ancient tree or the face of rock. He who makes it lifts his arms wide, his hands on some slight projection or in some hollow, not gripping. His breast heaves up and drives forward, as if into the hardness of rock-face or tree. But only the breast lives, except for the arms loosely stretched. The legs are unflexed, knees yielding a little and resting on the bulk of the object. The face has no expression, the eyes closed or without focus.

'And, fourth, there is that Gesture of conscious prostration. There is not essentially a seeking for rest. A man lies full length on the earth, wholly yielded, but in full command of his strength. His face is pressed to the earth, buried in the cool grasses which fret on his cheek. The face's expression will be slight, the lips dull. But the eyes may well have a strict concentration, only partially realised.

'There are these four Great Gestures. They are cardinal to the extent of our emotion and thought, indeed to the whole of life. And the man who has finally lost either the power or the desire, the need, to make any of these is himself lost.

'He is also, perhaps, a completely civilised man. For these four Gestures were equally cardinal to the men who fled from the glaciers, men whose world was entirely different from ours, both texture of soil and air and the earth's structure, both *animals and birds, insects and vegetation. They are the first Affirmations. They represent four Conceptual Nodes, at which Man's infinitely complex relation to the phenomenal world is drawn to Crisis and made articulate in complete Organic Symbol. There are other gestures, endlessly graded, endlessly combined and interwoven in their tens and hundreds and thousands, but all are related to these four Nodes. These are uncomplicated, and these alone are entire. They are the carnal-spiritual, the organic Lenses, which focus—ultimately, perhaps, at a single point—the light which radiates from universal flux, from this immeasurable Vital Sea and its infinite possibilities in Significance, this, unsoundable and uncontrollable, on which, for the most part, we merely drift, content in mere drifting, until some intense disharmony of relation forces us either to realisation, to admission and mastery, or to denial, a defection and a partial death. And the endeavour of realisation forces us to one or other of these four Cardinal Gestures. But this is metaphor, only.*

'One of these Gestures is commonly regarded as the Attitude of Prayer. But all are equally attitudes of prayer. Yet, in truth, if by prayer we mean only supplication, then none of these is wholly for prayer. None is made in supplication, in simple desire. In each there is desire, but there is also knowledge of fulfilment. Desire forces us towards these Great Gestures, but the spontaneous Gesture, fully made, tells, already, that our desire is fulfilled. It is fulfilled by being made articulate in the Gesture.

'The first of the four, that in which a man directs his body upward, presents a craving for strength, but it presents also the realisation of strength. He will make this Gesture, perhaps, at the crisis of sorrow. Or he will make it in the highest endurance of beauty. In either case, strength is added to him, both to his thought and to his action, and he may feel immediate compulsion to violent bodily movement, to tire the body and leave

thought free to enjoy its new power. The second, that of the bowed head and then of kneeling, is describable in the same terms, except that there seems to be a different craving and a different renewal. The meaning is different. The sorrow and the awe that force a man to this Gesture will arise from a different order of relations with external Significance, with Vital Otherness, relations, apparently, of a gentler order. Of two men who have suffered equal loss or equal abasement, one will be forced into the First Gesture, one into the Second Gesture. Of two men stricken by the same lurid sunset in the same high mountains, the one will strain his body upward with fierce effort, and the other will kneel. These two Gestures must seem to us the Articulate Poles of our complex interpenetrable life, the North and the South. By the same analogy, the Third and the Fourth Gestures will define, together with—and where?—some third point, the locus of a circle drawn away to East and West. But this conception must not be elaborated. It is sufficient to understand that these two, also, are at once Gestures of Desire and Fulfilment. In the Third Gesture, a man extends his arms loosely and asserts only the breast. It seems the Gesture of Will—a troubling of will, a symbolic declaration of will and a strengthening, or perhaps a redirection, of will. It is made, commonly, when some strong desire has long persisted towards unfulfilment. The Fourth Gesture seems to have greatest complexity. It presents a desire to be free of will, to forget the ruthlessness of desire. But it takes subtlety from the fact that here, too, is strengthening, and so there can be no entire submission or self-abasement. It is best seen as all complexities of weariness articulate and made free in simple utterance. It is above all the Gesture of Peace.

'But these phrases are finger-posts, only, and no more should be asked for. No verbal description must be imposed, substituted for intrinsic significance. For these Gestures are greater—they are

more completely articulate—than all figurations of words and all conceptual thought. The Seventh Symphony of Beethoven could more easily and more properly be defeated with verbo-conceptual formulæ. We can assert only that there is desire and fulfilment, strain and release, Articulation of Crisis, a pressure upon the quick nerves of basic life, of Otherness. We can relate circumstances, also. But, beyond this, we can declare nothing, without danger of denial, of breaking up, in thought, what is in itself profoundly integral and of working serious loss upon ourselves. What is important is to know that Man fittingly makes the pure and complete form of the Great Gestures only in solitude. The sharing of Crisis is dangerous. Each Gesture must draw to simple focus the relations between a single complex organism and the complex whole of Vital Otherness. The close presence, the interposition of Another, of one more urgent organic lens, may deflect some significance of relation, forbidding the clear Articulation of Crisis and preventing its natural fulfilment.

'For the Great Gesture is Man's spontaneous Æsthetic. In poem or in symphony, the artist, with patient labour, directs his gathered comprehension, his Mastery of Otherness, into grooved yet fluid concept: all art, we say, aspiring to the Condition of Music. But when, in solitude and in silence, the relentless Soul of the World, which is carnal, rushes upward into the Body of Man, which is spiritual; then, from that troubled complexity of carnal-spiritual organism, he shapes without deliberation, the clear Gestural Lens and finds release and fulfilment in its focus. And silence is made articulate. For a brief moment, Man is become Organic Poem.'

Most of which—though I shudder at the dreadful verbal debauchery and the faintly nauseating Yogi-bogey flavour—I still find convincing, as metaphor. . . . At any rate, the posture—I am calling it a gesture—of kneeling is acknow-

ledged as in some way valuable and efficacious throughout History and throughout the world. And that of 'tense
maximal erectness' is not only of impressive force as a
kind of climax-posture in the playing of Tragedy, but, it
may be remembered, was brought in, as a nobler posture
than that of kneeling, in D. H. Lawrence's Quetzalcoatl
ritual: one more, then, of Lawrence's grand half-discover-
ies. More apparently homely instances will doubtless occur
to the reader. He may feel a muscular, a kinæsthetic reminiscence of at least the tendency to draw the whole body
into the focus of some form of one or another of these four
cardinal gestures, in a moment either of unbearable clog-
ging of the faculties or of the intense and sudden experience (with suitable apologies to Dr. Richards) of Beauty.
And that without any previous reckoning (though, in our
self-consciousness and self distrust, the act is quickly
rationalised thus) that the gesture was, as we say, 'appropriate', without, indeed, any deliberation at all. . . .

It is, as it seems to me, a neglected matter of great importance. And—inexplicable, I think, in naturalistic terms
—it has some mystical implication which none of our religious terminologies is quite adequate to expound. But
this is not of immediate relevance. What I wish to establish, here, is quite simply, that these gestures are cardinal
to a fundamental human mode of articulation, that they
do not imply deliberation or anything that can properly
be called purpose and—as end-products, in the same order
as those of the recognised arts—that they are expressive
(not productive, but expressive in the full sense that they
are necessary and underived—as it were coincident or even
consubstantial—expressions) of achievements of peace,
release, new poise, harmony (these are metaphors), in

conditions, in complexes of experience, operative—and therefore with some violence—in the whole human organism and in all its parts.

Art, we may take it, has, at all times, had ritualistic functions, greater or less according to the closeness of its alliance with that range of cohesive beliefs and attitudes which constitutes the religion of a society. And a fairly thorough case can be made out for the belief that all Ritual and all art arise, by a continual process of differentiation, from the two primitive and fundamental modes of articulation—vocal and gestural—thus briefly enough described. But it is not supposable—and the caution is particularly necessary in considering the gestural mode—that either mode is ritualistic, at all, in origin. Gesture may be taken to precede Ritual of any kind, Ritual being the deliberate practice of Gesture when, with the growth of self-consciousness, its direct relation to desirable states is perceived. And there is every psychological, if no archæological, reason to suppose that Ritual itself precedes Belief, which may be considered as the post-factum rationalisation of Ritual, though forms of belief, once established, do, in the historical period, tend, in their turn, to determine ritual forms. This, as an historical thesis, needs to be argued at great length if it is to be freed of the air of fanciful hypothesis that it doubtless has when thus briefly stated. But once again, the only conviction desired, for the moment, is for the beliefs that art originates in acts of completer spontaneity than even the most long-sighted anthropologies can logically reach, that these acts, whose operation is essentially that of the most highly developed art-forms, precede both the ritualistic and the communicative functions of art and that bodily posture and vocal noise (not originally and not necessarily now functioning as forms of speech) are the most primitive and the most forcibly conditioned materials of art, so that, in a good many ways, all the 'significance' of the other arts rests, finally, on the inherent significance of pure physical impulses.

Taking this last formula down several tones in pitch, we have the simple assertion, which nobody has ever questioned, that singing and dancing are the basic arts. But we have also the assertion that Song and the Dance, in themselves and without any intrusion of extrinsic rational significances, represent—or are—processes operative in our experience at a depth or with an immediacy (according as we prefer spatial or temporal metaphor) inaccessible to the other arts. And, although nobody could doubt it who had both danced or sung and made poetic, pictorial or musical compositions, with equal compulsion and equal skill, yet this assertion has never entered into the deliberations of critics and æstheticians. New and useful material, then, is available to Æsthetics and Critical Theory, as a whole, from a study of the characteristics of singing and dancing: not as elements in elaborate hybrid art-forms, but as organic processes, as modes and techniques, in themselves, of articulation. This constitutes a Human Approach to Art. And the material most easily available—most useful, therefore, to these mere beginnings—will be found in a general effort to disengage the basic contrasted qualities of Eastern and Western Dance and Song, as these are displayed in their respective means of voice-production and muscular control.

But we have to be careful—especially with the Western Dance, the Ballet—that it is the essential thing, not its extrinsic attributes, that we are considering. We have to consider, as purely as possible, what the Dance is for the Dancer. As spectators, we are, for the most part, absorbed in the contemplation of a fusion—not merely a mixture— of visual and aural arts: elaborate music and elaborate pictures, fused together in such a way that the human pictorial elements behave, as I said, in the Manner of Music. Appreciation of the Dance itself must, to be pure, be purely nervous and muscular. Visual appreciation will not do. An arabesque is not primarily a visual form. It is not ⊤ or ⊱ embroidered with meat. Rather, it is what you feel like when your body tends towards these forms or when, by proxy, you contemplate such tensions in the Dancer, with the utmost inscape. And probably only those completely familiar with particular ballets, those who have completely exhausted for themselves the aural and visual interest of the particular ballet in progress, are capable of appreciation in fairly pure terms of this nervous dynamic. Having attained this agreeable state, by much attendance at Covent Garden, Sadler's Wells or the Ballet Club (better still, though, in the Classroom), and having had some taste, also, of Hindu or Javanese dancing,[3] we can then permit ourselves to figure out the main essential character- istics of the two, proceeding, then, for more substantial evidence, to do a like office for Song.

---

[3] Uday Shankar's art is pure enough, despite its assimilation of some Western tricks of presentation. The Javanese Prince Raden Mas Jodjana, however, might be a more excellent image to have in mind.

Plate 5. *Ardjuna.* (The Ideal Warrior.) Raden Mas Jodjana. *Franz Hals Photograph.*

The Flesh Made Word

André Levinson was, I suppose, the first to understand the significance of the 'outwardness' of Ballet, the whole basis of its Technique and Style, and he has contrasted it splendidly with the incoiling, the sustained reference to an 'inner ecstasy', of the Eastern movements: of the characteristic Spanish movements, too, which are predominantly Eastern in origin. In Ballet, the limbs are, as it were, developed and unfolded from the trunk. It is the continual outward extension from a focal point. In the Eastern Dance, everything coils inward. 'Les bras, en s'encurvant, enveloppent le torse.' But Adrian Stokes will provide us with a more vivid text. After setting out to assess the 'æsthetic significance' of the 'turned-out' basis of all Classical Ballet, the value of the five positions, and after charming us with some of his most careful and sensitive prose, he exhorts us to

'*Compare this sublime fulfilment, this perfect intercourse expressed in planes, with the progressive spirals of Spanish dancing that betray its Oriental ancestry or with the coils of mesmeric tension which the Indian or Javanese dancer builds up and with the same form expends. . . . The dances of other civilisations seem to us to express foremost the absorption of strength, the building up of a reserve of vitality, a kind of inner recreation. There are dances that denote the expenditure of energy: but one is still conscious that behind the movements of such dances the dancer is drawing to himself the strength of the outside world, appropriating the life of animals or of the fields, or feeding upon a cultural heritage, himself its god. Such dances symbolise an intensification of the human mystery, the wrapt human power of absorption alternating with expenditure. The more typical European forms of the dance are exactly the opposite: they show a dissolution of mystery, they express passion in terms of a uniform corporeal outwardness.'*

Mr. Stokes's statement is, I think, the perfect statement of the pure æsthete's response to that visible difference of muscular style with which concern is, here, though I wish he had acknowledged the debt to Levinson. And he did lead up to his statement from a consideration of the primary aspect of Ballet, the basis of its system of muscular control, the turning out of the whole of the legs and thighs at an angle of ninety degrees. Yet it is necessary to stress 'visible', to stress the fact that Mr. Stokes is concerned with the contrast only as a contrast of visual forms. The consequence is he has not let it appear that the forms of the Eastern Dance are equally related to (dependent on, ultimately) an equally characteristic muscular habit. The religious symbolism, the directly ritualistic nature of Oriental dancing, its cosmic significance, as expressed through the range of Mudras, traditional gestures, is bound to be more apparent to Western eyes. But (I speak as one who has tried, for many hours before a mirror, to imitate Uday Shankar's lateral neck-movements) the 'mere' technique, the 'mere' muscular accomplishment involved, though less spectacular, is no less significant than that which Tamara Toumanova requires, to give us a good Aurora. And significant in this sense. . . . It represents a natural mode of post-gestural articulation for the East or, referring back to the note on Behaviourism, a basic mode of controlled Emotion (not 'of controlled expression of Emotion').

But the significant characteristics of this system of muscular control? I would put them in the keeping of these two abstract nouns: Minuteness and Separateness. 'Minuteness' implies that—by comparison with Ballet—the component physical acts of any piece of Oriental dancing are the result of controlled exertion of very small groups of muscles. 'Separateness' implies that these minute component physical acts are considerable as significant in themselves: not (though several may be performed simultaneously) as cohering in the significance of a single broad movement of the whole body. In the common representations of Siva, as Nataraja, Lord of the Dance, for instance, the Mudras, the gestures, the symbolic forms, of his four or six hands are related to each other only in a literary, not a plastic, relation. They are words, strung together. Plastically, they are separate. According to Western notions, indeed, the plastic form of these statues, as wholes, is bad. No good Western sculpture would evolve such forms And, together, 'minuteness' and 'separateness' imply this general view: that the Eastern body, in its condition of maximal articulatory, expressive and finally communicative power is concerned with itself as the centre and field of interrelations of muscular acts; whereas the Western body, in its equivalent condition, is concerned with itself rather as a component unit, as the vehicle of a single act, interrelated or potentially interrelated, in a broad external field, a broad movement of choregraphic logic (of which there is almost none in the Eastern Dance), with the articulatory, expressive and finally communicative acts of other bodies.

Evidently, the character of this statement depends on a monistic view: that Body and Soul are coëxtensive, that 'physical' attributes or qualities, disengaged and described as such, are not different from or, at least, are exactly correspondent with 'spiritual' or 'mental' attributes and qualities. Granted this (though I believe restatement is possible in terms of other metaphysical views), a quite familiar group of equivalences works itself out from a quite new centre. The contrasted 'spiritual' characteristics of East and West are seen to be correspondent with, if not to derive from, their contrasted 'physical' habit. Thus. . . .

The East : The West : : Introversion : Extroversion : : Concentration : Expansion : : Comprehension : Community : : Centripetal : Centrifugal : : Contemplation : Action : : Thought : Feeling : : Hamlet : Quixote : : Subjective : Objective : : Speculative : Critical : : Hermit : Preacher. . . .

Etc., etc., until we argue up to a point at which we see that the Eastern soul (the Eastern body, in fact) is naturally pantheistic. . . . It holds itself, that is to say, at once an element and an epitome of all Godhead, whereas the Western soul (or body) must, of its nature, project a God beyond and above itself, with Whom, objectively, in certain kinds of act, it may establish real and sensible contact, which is Theism. Theism and Pantheism, then, are considerable as the final rationalisation of psycho-physical habits, deriving from the deliberate performance, the partial rationalisation, which is, in the given sense, the phase of Ritual, and constituting, themselves, the phase of Belief.

But this, a second time, takes the argument to a metaphysical plane that it need not reach or, with so many omissions, should reach. In these general notes, I am concerned only that such metaphysical implications (explications, perhaps) should appear possible, not entirely fantastical, and the one fact required to be accepted is that there is this relation, an important, a fundamental, an essential relation, between the general mental, psychical, spiritual, cultural characteristics assigned, by common agreement, to that undefined entity, the East, and a basic physical habit, its muscular style, and that the Western muscular habit, focused in Ballet to the highest possible degree, is no less, in its own right, related to whatever may be thought most significant in the whole culture of the West, if not in a causative, at least in an all-comprehensive mode. That, surely, is enough refutation of any who argue that the Dance as Pure Style is insufficient and who want to overlay it with extraneous literary and pseudo-religious 'significance', who want Ballet, for instance, to compete with Drama? Ballet, itself, without representational interest of any kind, is one epitome of the total history of the West. The pure devoted practice of it, therefore, not attempting to deviate from, but only to fulfil, to enrich, Tradition, is enough. Style for Style's sake, in the Dance, is not the same ideal at all as Art for Art's Sake, elsewhere. Style, in The Dance, is all-comprehensive. It contains the whole riches of a whole experiential order. Human significance resides in more than general ideas. Perhaps in general ideas least of all. . . . In Spinoza's metaphysic—in Blake's, in Lawrence's, if any of these had followed his thought through to the end—Body is consubstantial with Soul. The body is spiritual, and the soul is corporeal. For the Western World, it is in Ballet that this corporeal soul seeks a first full realisation.

This on the side of Gesture, of gestural articulation, of what we are essentially concerned with. . . . To complete the general argument, we can follow the same terms through on the side of vocal articulation. And exactly the same contrasts hold. Both by natural untrained habit and by traditional sophisticated culture, the production of the voice in the West tends towards its complete, shall we say, Exposure. That is to say, the voice is felt to be most pleasing, understood, also, to be best-produced, when all its potential sonority and richness in harmonics, upper partials, overtones, is realised. And this realisation necessitates that the whole of the body shall play its greatest possible part in the production of the voice: that, apart from the maximal chest (contralto and bass) or mask (soprano and tenor) resonance, the attempt to secure full sonority and richness in harmonics shall govern and determine the whole configuration of the body's stresses and relaxations, no less in the stance of the limbs, than in the carriage of head and torso. In the East, on the other hand (and, as with dancing, the East, here, must be taken to include among other folks, the Flamenco of Spain), the correct voice is a withheld voice. The completely 'white' tone is aimed at, and this (though its volume may be no less) is non-sonorous, is as free as possible from harmonics.[4] Furthermore, the Western production achieves a voice which will 'blend' to the utmost with other voices, while the Eastern voice is calculated not to 'blend' at all. To such an extent does this difference hold that, though individual 'quality' may be no greater in the one case than in the other, the choir, as understood in the West, is impossible in the East. Among a hundred Oriental singers, screaming together (as it necessarily seems to Western ears) in unison, every single voice remains unaffected by the rest. The voices are only added together, not fused. There is mixture, but no

---

[4] Whether there can be some unapparent actual physiological difference, I do not know. But it is true, or almost true, that the 'white' tone is impossible to the Westerner: in the sense, at least, that the attempt to produce it tends to strain and inflame the Western larynx and vocal cords.

compounding. A hundred European voices could, of course, be picked to blend so perfectly that, at a reasonable distance, no plurality of voice could be distinguished at all. This, at any rate, is the condition envisaged in Western vocal culture. And these two ranges of tendencies do so divide the world that we speak legitimately of the East and the West, without important sub-division. There are national differences. The Flamenco sings differently from the Japanese, the Bengali, perhaps, from the native of Madras. And there are perceptible differences between an Italian, a German, a Russian and, say, a Welsh tenor. But the envisaged, the ideal conditions are only two. The more perfect a singer is, the more nearly are his national characteristics neutralised, so that Chaliapine, for all his devotion to his native Russian music, could hardly be distinguished, vocally, from a German, an Italian or a West Riding bass of equal individual excellence.

B. *The Organisation of the Arts*

All this has bearings, evidently, on every form of art and, in fact, on every order of human activity, rather than specifically and exclusively on the Dance. Conversely, however, as I was careful to point out in the very earliest pages of my book, the whole of life hangs together so completely, and the Dance is so profoundly rooted in the whole of life, that Ballet alone can be fully understood only by reference to every other order of human activity. All these general critical implications must, then, without exception, bear intimately on Ballet. So I may be excused for seeming, still, to digress. That the digression is not impertinent digression, or fruitless, will, I hope, appear.

First, then, I do suppose an organic development of Music, Poetry and Plastic from the two primary modes of vocal and gestural articulation: that this development constitutes, in the East and in the West, alike, the basic Cultural Tradition, whose operations I tried to describe in Chapter II, and that, in both Eastern and Western traditions, all general characteristics of the arts, now, in their present most elaborate forms, are directly related to (made possible, determined by) characteristics of the primary articulatory modes. To be aware of the existence of such relations must, therefore, in itself, be of great negative critical importance, if only because it precludes false idealistic and a-prioristic approaches to the arts. And it is my own belief that the examination of these relations in detail —to give them positive critical bearing—is the most important task that Æsthetics and Critical Theory can at present undertake. But before any comprehensive critical apparatus can be evolved in these terms, it will be necessary to formulate clearly an historical view of the Gesture-Ritual-Belief development; of the passage from Articulation to Communication, studied psychologically; of the exact nature of correspondences between 'physical' movement and 'mental' state, so hopelessly obscured by many centuries of the use of dualistic terminologies; and a great deal more, none of which there is space for, here.

Meanwhile, we are enabled to make several restatements of characteristics of our own Western tradition, as a whole. Extroversion and Sonority being its dominant characteristics, we can look upon phases of unusual Introversion, non-

Sonority, Minuteness and Separateness (in a general way, atomisation of the materials of art) as representing, metaphysically, an Easternising. And we ought to look for corresponding modifications of muscular and vocal habit. Thus, Europe is almost entirely extrovert, with small significant breaks, until the latter half of last century. Deliberate intellectual extroversion, in Poetry (as opposed to spontaneous, emotional, romantic extroversion), culminates in the eighteenth century; and it is at this time, too, that the ninety-degrees turned-out positions in Ballet, finally developed, becoming text-book rules somewhere about 1780; while Song reached its fullest Sonority, its fullest realisation of the possibilities of the voice (equals the human body as a voice-producing instrument) as such, in the Italian Opera and the Handelian Oratorio.

The (metaphysical) Easternising, in our own time, must similarly be seen to reveal itself not so much in the deliberate importation of influences from the East (though there is this geographical Easternising, also)—the study of Eastern thought, the use of Eastern subject-matters, the use of Eastern gestures in Ballet and of Eastern modes in instrumental music—as in the fact that Poetry and Music, generally, cultivate all possible subtlety and evasiveness, both in rhythm and imagery (in Music, evocation), so that anything 'four-square' is abhorred; that painters and sculptors tend either to obscure their conceptions and bury them as deeply as possible in the material or to select for exposure an ultra-stylised minimum of their features; that Sonority and Breadth are, above all qualities, shunned, alike on the stage and in private speaking of Poetry; that vocal composition aims exclusively at expressive subtlety (which is non-vocal, even anti-vocal), Handel being finally negated by Hugo Wolf; that, singing in his bath, the contemporary European will emit a breathy croon (considerable as an equivalent of the 'white' tone) instead of a hearty bellow; that both our speech and our gait are increasingly minced, so that to speak audibly or to walk as though intending to reach a destination strikes us, now, as primitive, comical or even affected; that our moral concern is with the concealed, the unconscious, rather than the manifest, the conscious, being[5]; that deliberate incantatory symbolism, in artistic practice, is accompanied, in the work of Dr. Richards (who is, as nearly as possible, I think, the type-mind of our time), for instance, by critical preöccupation with the subjective process, the inward effects.

And so on. . . . These facts seem to me necessary reflections of the decay of a Western order of society, apt for relation to some such comprehensive dialectic of decay as the Marxian (itself a symptom in the same kind): the destruction of the efficiency of our rituals, which include speech habits, dress fashions, etc., as well as the arts, as the central socio-religious conception in which they cohere and which they serve becomes self-contradictory. But that is another line of talk, altogether. And the Westernising of the East (of which the importation of the empirical sciences constitutes only a small part) would be yet another. And they would be negative lines of talk. The important positive showing of such new arrangements of evident facts is of the absolute coherence and comprehensiveness of cultures and of the whole bodies of their art.

---

[5] The metaphysical implications of psycho-analysis (all the schools), it may be noted, are pantheistic.

The Organisation of the Arts

A culture which is not absolutely cohesive is a culture in decay. And more obvious symptoms of decay than those I have listed are, on the one hand, the gross over-assertion of Personality and, on the other, an unnatural atomisation of the forms of art and the isolation of specific compounds of these in air-tight compartments. A healthy culture is almost entirely impersonal. Its art is communal and comprehensive. There is little scope for personal idiosyncrasy. The cathedrals of Medieval Christendom are anonymous. We do not know who were their architects. Medieval Painting, Music, Poetry, also, are anonymous. A few names that we have, unearthed here and there, by scholars, are commonly problematical, and certainly we know more names of minor officials than of major poets. Only with the onset of the Humanist Renaissance do we meet The Artist, and Chaucer is our first Poet writ large. In the Middle Ages proper, artist was simple artisan. That he served capital Art with passion, with high and difficult skills, with stern patience, we cannot doubt. But he got no spurring from prospects of Glory nor even, it seems, much immediate reward.

To-day, we are so far sunk in ourselves that, meditating on such things, we are simply puzzled. That a man should make a cathedral and not seek to put his name down on the time-list seems, to us, an appalling piece of carelessness. That men should acclaim some swaggering bombard-baron and not fête their artists seems, to us, barbarous. Yet this, surely, and not our modern condition, in which every two-penny-ha'penny piece of verse or prose must be covered by its author's name, if it is to be read at all, is the normal condition. A high art, by any standards, goes back, with the Sumerians, as far, to our certain knowledge, as

151

3500 B.C. Yet there are no names of artists until the Glory that was Greece becomes uncomfortable. Exquisite work was done by Egyptian artists in tombs where even the contemporary eye was not expected. And the major art of India is anonymous even in modern times. The ages in which artists have claimed substantial public recognition, much less pronounced for 'immortality', cover a quite insignificant piece of time. Only in the Modern World is it Personality, in art as in business, that counts. Only for a little while have we committed the monstrous indecency of publishing our poets' love-letters.

What is it, then, in the nature of a society, a culture, which determines that sublime art shall be produced in complete obscurity, that passionate art shall be produced with decent reticence, that merely interesting art shall be produced with much gesticulation? I suggested an answer, already, in some historical remarks about dancing in the Ancient World. And any answer, certainly, must be in terms of function. We shall surmise that an anonymous art is, in some way, intrinsic to the fundamental needs of the society out of which it grows, that an art whose instruments are named with honour may be a vigorous and wholly valid art and yet is external to the deeper social movements, and that a highly self-conscious art is a functionless art, the produce of men who, as creative workers, are set apart from Society as a whole.

Sure enough, until Athens first cast up great names, art, in the Ancient World, was an integral service of Religion. So it was, too, in the close-built socio-religious structure of Medieval Europe. And so it has been in modern India. To the Hindu, art is one means of peeling away Maya, the Appearance, and of fixing in durant symbol some facet of immanent Godhead, the Reality. The Artist, until very recently, has been simply a craftsman, attached to the temples. Art has been hereditary, a caste function, working by traditional canon.

But we do not solve our problem by saying that in all times, except a few intruded centuries of self-conscious-ness, Art has been the servant of Religion and that anony-mous art is essentially religious art. For what do the terms mean? Surely, though I have denied it, Blake's art is essen-tially religious, in all the most important senses? So is the art of D. H. Lawrence. And these are far from anonymity. Perhaps 'hieratic' is a fitter term than 'religious' for the great ages of unsigned art. It is not true, except in purely political senses, that Sumerian or Feudal or Hindu art is more wholly the expression of a religious conception than that of Lawrence or Blake, Nietzsche, Dostoevsky, Keats, or of any artist powerful enough and resolute enough to build up his individual life within a religious conception. The difference is that Babylonia, like Medieval Christen-dom, like Classical Hindustan, had a religious conception equated to the societal conception, the political concep-tion. Society moved within the religious framework, which was a binding all-comprehensive ethic, both an in-dex and a sanction for all activity. There was no separation of Religion from Philosophy and Science, of Art from Politics and Public Entertainment, no division of Truth into many notional categories. There was one ideological framework for all processes of living. And Art was Ritual. Art is always that, but here it was Ritual for a truly welded and whole society, not for the individual or the coterie or the class. It was the heraldry of a fully integrated public mode of belief and behaviour. This is the very definition of a culture, a whole culture, and within such a culture, Tradition defines itself, in practice. To-day, Tradition is a subject for metaphysical discussion: for the simple reason that it no longer works. And our culture—if we may still claim to have or to be one—is more closely defined by dress fashions than by forms of art.

In our time, Art is the Reductio ad Absurdum of itself. Less epigrammatically, contemporary works of art and the relations between Art and Society are such as to render untenable any hypothesis singly proposed for the Nature and Function of Art. Even the con-committal Marxian view would need to be thoroughly overhauled and redialecticised before application. In other circumstances, Art may well be a reflection of Ruling-Class Ideology, but the position of the Superstructure becomes rather precarious when there is no body of people sufficiently large, homogeneous and cleanly stratified to be described as a class at all, and when those groups which are least equivocally said to rule have no ideology comprehensive enough to need or even to permit reflection in Art. It is not that Society has ceased to be interested in Art, but simply that cultural feeling tends to base itself, by preference, on the sentiments of the stock exchange and to find adequate ritual expression in the kaleidoscopic pageantry of dress fashions or, to the extent that artistic activity has a cultural role at all, in certain mushroom art-forms explicitly recognised as pure diversion, so that Art proper has no internal function, but becomes a branch of the tourist industry.

Among artists and, to some degree, among cultivated people in general, there is a feeling that such a state of affairs is unsatisfactory. And yet, logical conclusion as this state is of the whole process of personalisation, very few people would whole-heartedly seek outlet by a return to cultural anonymity. They would feel such return to be a complete negation of art: as, indeed, it is, for art as we know and consider it means the near traditional hinterland, only, becoming steadily more barren as it approaches the present sea-board.

Putting aside, however, the fact that so many artists, to-day, are more concerned to be artists, to be poets, to be painters, than to create works of art, the immediate question for serious people would normally be whether anonymous art is likely to be intrinsically superior to signed art. But that is an impossible question. There are no standards for comparing the Opus 111 with a Sumerian statue, and, in any case, Beethoven represents, historically, a mere phase in the process of transition from Ur to George Bernard Shaw. The question must be proposed more broadly. Will anonymous art tend to define a culture more generally pleasing to persons of æsthetic interests? And there it is possible to answer with a confident affirmative. Anonymous art is necessarily art subdued to a central non-æsthetic purpose, a social or socio-religious conception. And, however much we, trained to think of Art in terms of Personality, to define Art, at least implicitly, as Self-Expression and to rate æsthetic values as somehow 'higher' than social values—however much we may resent the thought of any such subordination of art to a non-æsthetic purpose, we must understand (though it may be contemptuously labelled hieratic, rather than religious, and political, perhaps, rather than hieratic) that this centripetal force makes Bad art impossible. Bad art is always to be defined as completely secular art and must, as such, be ruled out of any cohesive cultural idea. True, this natively artistic argument for anonymity is purely negative. But it is cogent, for the evil symptoms, to-day, are not in the lack of good Art so much as in excess of the bad. And it is doubtful whether any positive argument, whatever, could be advanced for signed Art, except by those whose definition of Art, in moments of complete and lucid honesty, would be the Activities of an Artist.

Which, certainly, is what Art means to most people, now. . . . Particularly is it so in the Dance. Apart from the free exhibitionists and outside Hollywood, there never was such a ramp of Personality as the present-day Ballet. By which token I fancy this present book can hardly do much to swell its author's royalties. . . . For, in these days, a pathological interest in remote personalities—a feminine or sub-feminine characteristic which ought never to enter into serious critical fields—is almost our master sentiment. The two dominant literary forms to-day are Biography and the Novel, the basic function of both of which is to make less wearing our bewilderment and self-contempt by 'taking us out of ourselves', on the one hand, and, on the other, by assuring and reässuring us—to bolster up our shabby self-esteem—that the great and successful, also, were, at heart, feeble, cunning and unfulfilled. A glut of Personality, everywhere. . . . Nothing but Personality. . . . Thousands of disgusting little egos crawling about, shrieking to be heard, each a law unto itself. . . . Every man his own philosopher. . . . One man one pub. . . . And books on Ballet, in particular, become best-sellers only by tapping all the sources of gossip and slaking our itch to see what weaknesses and mere charms the dancers have, in private life: though the Dancer, most significantly, in this loud limp ungraceful age, ought to seem an impersonal, single and ideal being, an embodiment of Pure Style and altogether a creature of the Theatre, who should never be seen, or even thought on, off a stage.

One day, we shall have to return to a degree of anonymity and health. That is certain. The return may, conceivably, be accomplished in purely political ways, through a form of Communism, perhaps. My own belief is that we shall not have social and cultural wholeness, again, until we are again a theocracy. But to get back to the Theatre. . . . It is evident enough, I fancy, that when Society is whole, is at one with itself, is not split and atomised by innumerable divisions of class, creed and education, then Art, also, will be whole. And, to a certain degree, all Art will be Theatre. The Theatre will be the focus of all the cultural activity of the community. There has to be a single focus, and, in vigorous communities, there has never been much of a gap between the Theatre and the Church. The Theatre has been almost identical with the Temple. And it has tended to subsume the totality of the community's practice, which is all ritual practice. This is the case in all healthy orders of society. And a few intelligent people, in our own supremely unhealthy order, are beginning to see it and to come to very definite conclusions about what must be done.

But we have to be very careful. It is fatally easy to come to definite practical conclusions: especially in large matters like Society, Culture, Art, which are too ill-defined and expansive to force us to immediate proof or disproof. Intelligence, sincerity and patience seem to come together only very rarely. And there is a quite fierce tendency, among the most highly intelligent and sincere minds of today, to envisage and strive towards the Theatre of the

Future in ways that (if there were any chance of strong enough numerical backing to make them socially effective, which there isn't) must inevitably destroy a great deal that is valuable. I may instance the practice of W. H. Auden, which, in itself, is fine and invigorating, but in its implications, quite appalling, and the critical writing of Herbert Read who, though one of the sanest people in this mad world, has been capable of suggesting that poets might save Society and their own souls by surreptitiously introducing a loftier tone into the music-halls. But, as one of the most intelligent and sincere of them all, and quite the least patient, we may take Michael Sayers, perhaps the best of our young dramatic critics and certainly one of the few contemporary writers worth disagreeing with.

I have quoted Mr. Sayers, already, in my first chapter, as one possessed of a quite straightforward contempt for Ballet. That quotation hardly does him justice. He has written on the Dance, once or twice, since then, with a considerable degree of appreciation and understanding. None the less, he is still Ballet's enemy. He is antagonistic to the Dance, as a whole, in a peculiarly insidious and dangerous way. And the measure of his enmity is the measure of his earnestness in the pursuit of a theory of the Theatre of the Future. That theory—as a representative theory—is worth examination in some detail.

'*Theatre is first of all a* synthetic *art—which means that its material is not homogeneous as in painting or literature. Second:* it presupposes an audience—and this means that it is not lyrical and subjective, but dramatic and communal (or social). A third point might be made, and equally emphasised: theatre remains undeveloped until it becomes synthetic. The fact that it is synthetic in nearly all primitive cultures (in Java, in early*

The Organisation of the Arts

Japan) presents us with the paradox that modern theatre must go backwards if it is to go on at all. We must go back to the old communal tradition of art where the impulse to make is immediately followed by the impulse to show and share. That is the essence of theatre—showing, sharing; and in our time creative theatricality can come only from those artists and critics who are sufficiently socially aware to feel the need to use their art in some way. T. S. Eliot recognised this when he affirmed that the best possible use for poetry was "in the theatre". If he meant in a poetic theatre I can no longer agree with him. The splitting up of theatre into many sorts of theatres results in unnecessary and bad introverted arts. Look at the poetic theatre after Shakespeare; the music theatre after Wagner; the dance theatre which has not been able to assimilate Noverre: all quite decadent, wasteful, useless. Only very restricted dramatic ideas can be expressed by Word alone, or Music alone, or Movement alone. The drama of this age of masses must be expressed by an art capable of using all these forms in combined effect.'

Those are Mr. Sayers's main positions. And most of them I applaud. But there is one inherent weakness, there, which flaws the whole theoretical structure based on these positions.

It is necessary, certainly, that we have a Theatre 'capable of using all these forms in combined effect'. But Mr. Sayers is not content with 'capable of'. He wants to make capability into obligation. At the back of his mind, evidently, was the more sweeping proposition that 'the drama of this age of masses must be expressed by an art which does'—always and everywhere—'use all these forms in combined effect'. Mr. Sayers, quite rightly, wants to see vigorous experimentation in synthetic theatrical forms. He is so impatient to see it that he will not allow anything not synthetic to be even legitimate. Everything must be composite, nothing single. And that, of course, is vicious nonsense.

The poetic theatre since Shakespeare is not decadent because it has become more purely poetic. It is decadent because the post-Elizabethan bourgeoisie has provided no audience for theatrical poetry: Poetry, in all its kinds, has become increasingly irrelevant to the intellectual and spiritual functioning of Industrial Capitalism. The music theatre since Wagner is not wasteful because Wagner wanted to isolate theatrical music. On the contrary, Richard Wagner was a synthetist after Mr. Sayers's own heart, and, according to his own theories, Mr. Sayers ought to applaud all the specifically post-Wagnerian developments. And J-G. Noverre was rejected, by the dance theatre, for the very good reason that he wanted to make the Dance literary and dramatic, at a time when the Dance was too vigorous to need bolstering up in any such fashion. Had he been living in our own time, Noverre would have been very popular. No, the trouble—and Mr. Sayers ought to know it better than I, for he is a Marxian—is with horizontal divisions of Society, not with vertical divisions of Art. The gap between the Theatre and the Stadium, of my second chapter, is essentially a sociological and not an æsthetic gap, as I think I made clear. The assimilation of the one to the other does not mean that we shall have to do *Les Sylphides* at Wembley Park or stage the cup-final at Covent Garden. The trouble is not that the different arts exist in isolation. They don't. Most of our present-day art-forms are composite. They are already synthetic. The important split is the split into distinct levels of appreciation. Taste, at every social level, is misconditioned by forms of education which allow and encourage all the stigmata of class-distinc-

tion and by the unspeakable propaganda-methods and techniques for the debasement of natural intelligence that are
cultivated by the Press, the Cinema, the B.B.C., etc.

In consequence, the composite art-forms which satisfy
one social layer are inaccessible to the other social layers,
above or below. Mr. Sayers enjoys the verse of T. S. Eliot
and Wystan Auden, the dancing of Kurt Jooss, the scenic
designs of somebody or other and the music of I don't know
whom, and would like to have all these things mixed together in the Theatre of the Future. The Man in the Street
enjoys the prose of Ethel M. Dell or J. B. Priestley, the
dancing of Ginger Rogers or Jessie Matthews, the music of
Albert W. Ketelbey or George Gershwin and scenic designs which are just like Nature, only bigger and better,
and he gets them mixed together, at the local cinema. Synthesis, certainly, is not our need, to-day. Nearly everything
we have, in any quantity, is synthetic, from education to
tooth-paste, from silk stockings and pearls to religious
exercise. In fact, if anything that is mere process can do us
any good, then analysis is more hopeful than synthesis. The
contemporary world is such a mess, such an overwhelming
synthesis, of confusion run into confusion, that some kind
of resolute purism, for the reëstablishment of clear outlines, seems to be the best idea that we can cultivate.

If we ever achieve that clarity, then, perhaps, we can
start talking about synthesis, all over again. But at all times,
even in an ideal society, a supreme social synthesis, it is the
clearly distinct forms which are most valuable. It is the impact of opposites which is fruitful, not of forms which are
nearly alike. Let the Dance be quite clearly distinct from
Drama, and the choregraphic stage and the dramatic stage,
in an harmonious society, will mutually heighten and clarify

each other's forms. And then they will be able to come together, at the right seasons, fruitfully. But make the Dance dramatic and Drama choregraphic. Melt down their forms, into indeterminacy, and blur their outlines. And they will spill over and flow into each other, like spilt pots of different synthetic treacles, and be as fruitful as the union of indeterminates usually is. I am not sure that Mr. Sayers' kind of synthesis in reality is much more, in fact, than a huddling together for warmth. What Mr. Sayers is really up to may be no more than the collecting together, for safety, of the very small contemporary forces of serious art, which do indeed seem as though they could no longer subsist in their own right. It may be only a regimentation of highbrows, against the enemy, or the crowding of them into an ark, against the Deluge.

In which case, I am inclined to shut one eye and throw in my lot with him. . . . But that pointing to Java as the glorious example, certainly (and Mr. Sayers has several times pointed to it so), is thoroughly unscrupulous. I have pointed to Classical India, myself, in a similar connection, but I was careful to stress more strongly the Western equivalents, of Classical Hellas and Medieval Catholic Feudalism. In actual fact, though the Javanese culture has never produced a distinct verbal Drama or a distinct and purely stylistic Dance, yet it has categories quite as exclusive. The splitting of the Eastern Dance-Drama, as a whole, into 'moods' or 'emotions' ('ragas', in Sanskrit[6])—and there

---

[6] Thirteen of them. . . . These are Sringara (Adi), Karuna, Dasya, Sakhya, Madhura, Vatsalya, Vir, Hasya, Adbatua, Bhayanaka, Raudra, Shanti, Bibhatsa: appropriate, respectively, to Sexuality, Compassion, Devotion, Fraternity, Conjugality, Parenthood, Valour, Mirth, Wonder, Awe, Terror, Peace, Phantasy. And these, with innumer-

are other divisions—is much more restrictive and purist than any systematisation we have in the West. Mr. Sayers doesn't really want the Javanese condition, though, or anything like it. That all art shall be religious ritual, that is excellent. That convergence of the arts on a single focus is precisely what I want. But it is a quite different thing from the convergence of the arts on each other, in an unfocussed fusion. The supremely important thing—the Temple, the focus—is lacking. Mr. Sayers is, I think, guilty of some intention, probably unrecognised by himself, to substitute the Theatre for all such forms of the Temple as should properly subsume the Theatre: of a wish to make Art—glorifying it beyond all that it can bear—a complete substitute, in itself, for all that goes under Religion. And this, apart from anything else, is (as T. E. Hulme pointed out) the final absurdity of Romanticism. It is what Jacques Maritain calls the 'deadly error'—that is, the mortal error, nothing less—of asking Poetry 'to provide the super-substantial nourishment of man'.

But let me repeat that—both in his own right and as the representative of greatly increasing tendencies—Mr. Sayers is one of the few contemporary critics worth quarrelling with. That is why I have found it necessary here, to examine him. These tendencies may presently become popular enough to be more than theoretically dangerous. And, if Mr. Sayers can become involved in such confusions, there's no imagining what sort of mess his colleagues' minds are in. Accordingly, when Mr. Sayers goes on about dancing, I am seriously worried. This kind of thing. . . .

---

able minor variants, are non-interpenetrable and rigidly associated with both place and season and specific musical accompaniments (in Sanskrit, 'ragas').

A Philosophy of Ballet

'*The Ballet is in a mess because it cannot resolve its own problem: to be, or not to be, expressive? The balletic dilemma being, that if it becomes expressive it must lose most of its style, and if it retains its style it cannot be expressive. . . . The Ballet is at a dead end: either it follows Jooss, and plumps for expressiveness, or else it returns to Cecchetti, and passes gracefully into the company of trapezery and tumbling. It can develop only within the dramatic theatre.*'

Which (written more or less directly against myself and in my own terms) draws such easy conclusions from such true and such acutely perceptive premises. . . . It is a fact. Ballet is in a mess. And it is in a mess because it cannot make up its mind. It wants to be more than Ballet. It wants to compete with Drama. It wants, in fact, to behave pretty much as Mr. Sayers would like it to behave. But it is precisely if it achieves these confused aims that the regression —a technical and stylistic regression, beyond Cecchetti— will ensue. And that will be the end of Ballet. What Mr. Sayers diagnoses is precisely what confounds the situation in and after Diaghilev, which I must presently go on to analyse. But the conclusion is a piece of quite inexcusable rhetoric. Therefore it can only, etc. . . . Q.E.D. . . . If that kind of flourish is, at this point, found convincing by my readers, without any further comment, then I have already wasted about fifty thousand words. Yet it is just such remarks that are being made, by the nicest and most intelligent people, all over the place.

That's enough of that, though. I have to come to my own analysis of the mess that certain aspects of Ballet are undoubtedly in. Here, I must simply reïnforce, from all the foregoing, my second main position: which is, as simply as possible, that the important thing in Ballet is Ballet. We have discovered enough 'significance' in the purely muscular and nervous bases of the Dance to be able to dispense, quite cheerfully, with anything but pure Style. We have resolved our initial paradox. It is precisely because Ballet 'arises in common organic processes' and needs, for its full understanding, 'reference to every other order of human activity' that it must be regarded, in the seemingly contrary sense, 'as an absolute and closed art'. So long as we set it against its full background and do not seek from it satisfactions that belong elsewhere, Ballet justifies itself completely. It is sufficient in itself. We don't need to express anything extrinsic at all. We don't need to enact great drama, nor to interpret the Cosmos, in a poetic way; though, of course, whatever drama, metaphysics and poetic imagery we do employ might as well be the best we can get. The important thing, in any elaborate structure, is the grading of values within it. And intrinsic values must dominate. In Painting, we allow the most important thing to be paint—in Music, notes. If the painter wants to paint a dancer or the musician to evoke the grace of one, it is still the paint and the notes that matter, not the dancer. So, when the painter and the musician are employed in Ballet, they must, in their turn be subordinated to the purposes of Ballet, of physical movement. It is necessary to stress this, again and again. Ballet audiences of to-day—including the critics—can be roughly divided into those interested in Music, who like their Music interpreted, à la Dalcroze, by physical movement; those interested in Pictures, who like their Pictures set in motion, because the damn things look so flat and lifeless in frames; those interested in Feminine or—more often—Masculine Beauty, which, apparently, they cannot find elsewhere.

A Philosophy of Ballet

And those who want Literature, but want it free of the struggle with a language gone mad. . . . These are both the most numerous and the most intolerable nuisance, partly because they assimilate the pure visualists and the pure auralists as well. I am indebted to Herbert Read for the suggestion that the present mass enthusiasm for Ballet is due to a loss of the feeling for words and is decadent in that sense. On the whole, I believe it is true, though I believe that it does not impugn Ballet, but only the modern literary ballets (of which the most literary, even though the latter has no stated programme, are Massine's two 'choregraphic symphonies', *Les Présages* and *Choreartium*). It is far too easy to generalise like that. It is as easy, say, and in precisely the same way, as it is to praise Diaghilev roundly for his lavish encouragement of the new painters and musicians, though this, as I shall try to show, has done quite as much harm as good to Ballet, pleasant as it was for the musicians and painters, as well as for the cosmopolitan dilettanti, Diaghilev's essential clientèle, who liked, as we all too easily like, to get through as much culture in one evening as possible, especially when it was fashionable culture.

I am not trying to argue—not at all—that Ballet must or will or can get along without good music, good painting or, for that matter, good literature. But it must, centrally and essentially, be free of these things. On the choregraphic stage, they must be subordinate. They must come and go, not settle in. In the logic, the choregraphic unfolding of a particular ballet, there must be absolute fusion and singleness. That is true. No element must be separate from another.

'*Ballet, viewed as a structure, a system of tensions, is human beings behaving in the Manner of Music. It is not a mixture of*

166

The Organisation of the Arts

Music and Pictures and, if you like, Acrobatics, but a fusion of these. It is human bodies, themselves constituting pictures, designs in Space, their separate movements interacting like musical phrases, like the idiom of a language, in such a way that the designs in Space become designs in Time, also, projected into rather than accompanied by the actual music of the orchestra, which itself, thereby, becomes spatially significant. And this makes up, as a single whole, the organic structure of life itself, simplified into manageable forms and making possible an immediate directness of response.'

But that singleness and resolved complexity of structure depends on a clear and definite grading. There are intrinsic attributes, and there are accidental attributes. And the single entity is not made by simply adding these together, in any kind of proportion. There is organic proportion. The tensions inherent in the Dancer's single body are the basic and essential material. Choregraphic form provides a system, a field, for the inter-operation of these tensions. And the rest is entirely subsidiary to choregraphic form.

It should be obvious, at any rate, that the best Ballet decor is not necessarily the best piece of Pictorial Art, nor the best Ballet music the best eight hundred bars of Music. The best Ballet music, hereto, has been Tschiakowsky's and Stravinsky's. Tschaikowsky was content to work in plain valse rhythms, most of the time, with nice pseudo-passionate rubato's occurring where necessary. And his only positive contribution was cleanly constructed melodies, with no pretence to cosmic inclusiveness, but just the apt tenderness or joyousness or grandiosity of mood. Stravinsky, being congenitally incapable either of constructing an original melody or developing a borrowed one, gave his choreographers (the scenario was often his own) a kind of rhythmic continuum, to evolve their forms in as they pleased, with a purely physiological rise and fall of intensity, girding at the solar plexus, the bowels or the spine, whichever was most appropriate to the dancers' activities on the stage.

And the best decor is that which provides a single sharp symbol for the Dance to expound, the best costumes those which, while according with the moods evoked by that symbol, do nothing to hide the lines of the choregraphic form. The lush decors of Leon Bakst are good, because they do nothing but represent Lushness, in one or another of its plain kinds. The best of all Ballet decors, though, is probably Joan Miró's for *Jeux d'Enfants*, of which the curtain consists of bold random daubs, on a white ground, of red, yellow, green, blue and indigo, given coherence by a simple superimposed pattern in black; the costumes, dominantly, of white head-to-foot woven garments, ringed or blobbed with the same primaries, like the paint on all good toys; and the backcloth of a combination of these with a bluish haze for a ground, where everything is slightly blurred, limp, disjointed—what the child's imaginings will be when the dream has run its course. But, when audiences are used to unit sets and the Cyclorama, on the dramatic stage, Ballet may well come to dispense with decor altogether, except what the lighting can provide. There is always irresoluble conflict between the round urgency of the dancers and the backcloth, which always keeps so stupidly, cynically, still and flat and limp. The stage on which there is dancing demands a three-dimensional shadowed image that can be made to pulse and harden and hover. It clamours for colour that is as vivid, quick, substantial, as the Dancer himself, clinging to him or setting its own movements against his, following and heightening his every change of rhythm and mood, intensifying the sheer muscular impact: images and colours, in fact, which are themselves alive. The Cyclorama can give us these—and will, when London managers wake from their long sleep.

So much, then, for the general modes of interdependence of the arts. . . . We have some apparatus, now, with which to examine the particular experimentations of Diaghilev and his successors. I am not implying that what I have argued out can possibly be thought to constitute a comprehensive critical equipment. Not in the least. . . , It is much too soon for us even to dream of an exact science of Ballet Criticism, even supposing that any criticism can ever be scientific. But we have certain definite principles and definite attitudes. We have enough equipment to make some show of understanding what Diaghilev was essentially up to: a matter which nobody has yet made much attempt to understand. And we have enough positive values to let us draw up—though without much detail—serious critical accounts, for the present and the immediate future.

V. Damages

A. Sergei Pavlovitch Diaghilev and the Aftermath

August 19th, 1929, The Death of Diaghilev: a date, in the thought of many, like W. A. Propert, to be put with 1815 or even 1066. . . .

'*He was buried in the cemetery of S. Michele at Venice, and there one day will stand the only tangible memorial to a man so unlike his fellows that we can find no parallel with which to compare him. . . . Diaghileff worked by no formula, had no method in his inspired intuition. His ear was familiar with all music, his eye trained to all beauty of form and colour. How could these endowments be passed on . . .? When he died, everything that was his died with him.*'

And to this may be added the remarkable words of Sergei Lifar, Diaghilev's last favourite, in a letter to Edith Sitwell, which Mr. Propert's book, on Diaghilev's second decade, quotes.

'*Il a emporté avec lui dans l'autre monde son secret magique de l'éternelle jeunesse. . . . Aujourd'hui, de l'au-delà, il voit devant lui l'infini de l'espace, du mouvement, de la forme . . . et je suis sûr qu'il possède ce talent d'être "là-haut" et sur la terre en même temps. Tel il fut dans sa vie. . . .*'

Which gives us, altogether, one of the two established views

Sergei Pavlovitch Diaghilev and the Aftermath

of Diaghilev: the view of those who, still dominated by the will of the undoubted colossus, must believe that Ballet owes all to him.

A second view gives us the colossal charlatan, embodying in himself, and prosecuting, all the more grandiose futilities of his time.

'*To the post-war intellectual snob all periods are equally* vieux jeu, *including his own, and it is only by a feverish rushing from one period to another that he can disguise from others and from himself his essentially static intelligence.* . . . *The most successful time traveller of our days was undoubtedly Serge Diaghileff, though it might be more accurate to describe him as a ubiquitous and highly efficient Cook's man to the time travellers, rather than a bona fide voyager.*'

Constant Lambert writes so with the courage of Percy Wyndham Lewis's convictions, and I would have quoted Mr. Lewis instead, but Mr. Lambert writes better. It is true Mr. Lambert's concernment is exclusively musical, as Mr. Lewis's is exclusively pictorial and literary. The one might well be colour-blind, the other tone-deaf, both of them empty of muscular images; and neither has yet produced any solid reason why an artist or an impresario should not time-travel, and make pastiche, if he wishes to. But the two together have defined a coherent attitude towards Diaghilev and all his works, and those who use their peculiar dialectic are necessarily convinced that Diaghilev's influence on Ballet was all bad.

Both the established views of Diaghilev, then, are distinguished by a lack of subtlety. And so would a third view be, a pseudo-view, which said that 'the truth probably lies somewhere between the two'. The full truth must certainly be one that includes the two (since they are, plainly, both temperamental and justified) and yet negates them both. In these subtle days, Diaghilev cannot be either hero or villain of the piece, but both, the piece itself, a great deal more and something less. So—on Diaghilev the man—let us have M. D. Calvocoressi, who seems admirably sane, though cautious.

'I found him to be a man endowed with a good deal of taste, but a taste so catholic and mutable as to be most disconcerting until one remembered that he was the type par excellence of the cosmopolitan—very cosmopolitan and very, very Russian. But he was endowed with both the will to do things and an extra-ordinary capacity for doing them.'

Or making other people do them. . . . And then it can be suggested, as a thesis, that Diaghilev's concernment was no more with Ballet than Mr. Lewis's or Mr. Lambert's is; that even his accidental influence on Ballet has been purely negative and yet that Diaghilev was something near the most important force in the Theatre of his time.

Evidently, this is a wanton and extravagant view, recommended only, on sight, by its originality. And Originality, as it is most understood, is one of the virtues with which this book itself has least sympathy. But I believe that a bare re-inspection of Diaghilev's career will show it to be a just view, if Ballet is taken to mean what I have made it mean. And it has to be noted, first that the young Diaghilev was a vague æsthete, simply, with wealth and a powerful personality and no particular interest in Ballet. Jacques-Emile Blanche gives him to us, in the Anglo-French Dieppe of the Beardsley and Yellow Book 'nineties (he was born in 1872), as 'a brilliant youth who bought his ties from Charvet, the smartest hosiers in Paris', could be 'by turns charming and sensitive and implacable as a tiger', was in-

terested in Beardsley, Conder and Masculine Beauty and
'had an almost superstitious faith in whatever seemed
original, new and unconventional . . . as, for instance, in
the theory that Surprise is the fundamental element in
æsthetic beauty and the inspirer of our highest emotions'—
in fact, 'the final word in elegance, a "dandy" to the tips of
his fingers; and there was no sign . . . to indicate in what
direction his career would turn, unless it was this taste for
what is new, this fickleness and this feverish impatience
which made him discard very quickly the things he had
once admired. . . .'

By the turn of the century, Diaghilev had, as we say,
made himself felt as a person in Imperial Russia. In his
own words—for which, also, I am indebted to W. A. Propert—

'*J'étais attaché pour missions spéciales au Directeur des Théâtres Impériaux depuis l'année 1899 jusque 1901. J'étais jeune et
plein d'idées. J'ai édité pendant une année l'Almanack des Théâtres Impériaux (c'était très joli). Je voulais tourner les théâtres
vers le chemin que je poursuis jusqu'à maintenant. Ça a raté. Il
s'ést produit un scandale phénoménal, interventions des Grands
Ducs et des Princes, des femmes fatales et des vieux ministres, bref,
pour me faire sauter, les différents gros personnages ont fait qua-
torze rapports à Sa Majesté l'Empereur. Pendant deux mois
Pétersburg ne parlait que de cette affaire. Grâce à elle le Directeur
des Théâtres Impériaux sauta lui-même immédiatement après moi.
À l'étonnement de la Russie bureaucratique une semaine après ma
chute, l'Empereur a donné l'ordre de m'attacher a Sa Chancellerie
Personelle. Bien-bitôt après j'ai quitté la Russie. L'Empereur ne
m'aimait pas, Il m'appellait "le malin" et une fois, Il dit a mon
cousin, Ministre de Commerce, qu'll avait peur qu'un jour je Lui
jouerais un mauvais tour. Pauvre Empereur, à quel point Son*

souci était mal placé! Il ferait mieux de reconnaître les gens qui
Lui ont vraiment joué le tour fatal.'

From this time, Diaghilev produced, abroad, Russian
Opera, Ballet and Concert Music, indifferently, being able,
till 1909, by favour of the Grand Duke Vladimir, to borrow
his artists and experts from the Russian Imperial Theatres,
instead of having to maintain them himself. With the Grand
Duke's death, this was no longer possible, and the Diaghilev Company proper was formed in 1909, making its
début, with Ballet, at the Théâtre du Châtelet, Paris.

At the beginning, Calvocoressi was in charge of the
music, Michel Fokine of the choregraphy and production.
Calvocoressi left in 1910, Fokine, finally, in 1914. It is
important that Fokine was in no sense a creature of Diaghilev. He was probably the greatest choregrapher that Ballet has had and, as such, really needs a substantial book to
himself. But it must be noted, here, that he was a mature
artist before the Diaghilev Company was born, taking from
Isadora Duncan, as I have said, all that was permanently
valuable in her work and clamouring already, in 1907, for
a Ballet which anticipated all that will be left of the Diaghilev productions. Here is Calvocoressi's word on his colleague:

'It was especially he who aroused my enthusiasm. . . . He
seemed to have a hundred eyes in his head. At an incredible
speed, he would go round each line or group in turn, showing one
dancer how to perform a step, correcting another one's attitude,
helping a third to understand the rhythm and phrasing of the
music. He had an unerring sense of construction as well as of col-
our and motion. I doubt whether, without him, Diaghileff's Ballet
could have come into being. . . . The way in which . . . he could
handle masses . . . rendered him incomparable and irreplaceable.'

174

Sergei Pavlovitch Diaghilev and the Aftermath

It is not noticeably unfair, indeed, to look upon Diaghilev, during this first phase, as business manager to the Ballet Fokine. New ballets by Fokine, from 1909 to 1914, were *Le Pavillon d'Armide, Prince Igor, Le Festin, Schéhérazade, L'Oiseau de Feu, Carnaval, Cleopatra, Les Sylphides, Sadko, Le Spectre de la Rose, Narcissus, Petrouchka, Le Dieu Bleu, Thamar, Daphnis and Chloë, Papillons, La Légende de Joseph, Midas* and *Le Coq d'Or*: a third of all the Diaghilev ballets and a list which includes almost all the Diaghilev survivors. And then, apparently, Diaghilev came to the conclusion that Western Europe was admiring Ballet, not Sergei Pavlovitch Diaghilev, and Fokine had to go.[7] He tried to form a company of his own, which might have carried Ballet continuously over, from the Russian School to our own time. But he did not find the means, and Diaghilev was left to comb together a long and perpetually changing run of musicians, painters and choreographers, in the manufacture of a kaleidoscope of synthetic theatrical entertainments where the Dancer's actual work became less and less important, though Diaghilev's feeling for Masculine Beauty, remaining unimpaired, made him very strenuously heighten its appeals and glamours.

But all this after another unbroken phase, a shorter one. . . . During Fokine's reign, the only non-Fokine Diaghilev ballets had been, in 1912 and 1913, Vaslav Nijinsky's three pieces, *L'Après-Midi d'un Faune, Le Sacre du Printemps, Jeux,* and Boris Romanov's *Salome*, 1913, with revivals of *Le Lac des Cygnes* and Coralli's even earlier *Giselle*. From 1917 to 1920, Diaghilev was almost as constant to Léonide Massine, as choreographer; and even with the settings, Leon Bakst

---

[7] It was also, of course, the affair Nijinsky.

was not relegated until 1914 or finally dropped until 1922. Massine did a few other ballets for Diaghilev's second decade and had done *Soleil de Nuit* in 1915, but the ballets of his sustained period may be listed, here, as *Parade, Contes Russes, The Good-Humoured Ladies, Les Jardins d'Aranjuez, La Boutique Fantasque, The Three-Cornered Hat, Pulcinella, Le Chant du Rossignol, Le Astuzie Femminile* and a revision of *Le Sacre du Printemps*: from 1917 to 1920—a period which had no other first productions except the Bluebird pas de deux, from *La Belle au Bois Dormant,* probably the most perfect set of dances Petipa ever composed. The main general importance of the change from Fokine to Massine must be seen as —for Diaghilev—a passage from Glamour to Sentimental Satire, from Romanticism to a clever Symbolism, and— for Ballet—a rejection of strictly classical dancing in favour of what was known, in Petipa's day, as character dancing. Fokine refined and built more closely the classical structures. Massine did the same for the folk-dance forms which had earlier been imported and stylised in Ballet. And the whole transition was, in effect, a shifting of stress from off Ballet and on to Theatre, from Choregraphy, finally, to Drama.

The most extravagantly popular dancers of this phase were Massine himself and the dainty Lydia Lopokhova, now the wife of J. M. Keynes, the economist, who proved herself more winsome to Diaghilev's audiences than any who had gone before. Nijinsky, whose supremacy as a dancer had not made him an efficient Master, had left before Massine's reign. But Karsavina was back, in 1919, for *The Three-Cornered Hat*. And then Massine went. Michel Larionov, who had already staged some of Massine's work, came along with a ballet, *Choût* or *Le Bouffon,* for 1921, worked up on music of Serge Prokofiev, from scenario and settings to choregraphic detail: a piece of work more notable for colour and noise than for anything else, for the most screeching harmonies possible, appealing to the spine both from the orchestra and the stage. *Cuadro Flamenco* followed, not a ballet, but an all-singing, all-dancing show done by a troupe of ten Spaniards with the help of Pablo Picasso. And the whole interlude came to a violent end with an amazing reproduction of *La Belle au Bois Dormant,* in full, the first Diaghilev show in which the man's crazy will to surpass in magnificence was fully let loose in pure pasticcio.

It will have been noted that Diaghilev had already revived *Le Lac des Cygnes, Giselle* and the Bluebird excerpts from the work now in hand. From the testimony of several of his colleagues, at this time, it appears that he had a notable fondness for Tschaikowsky's music. He had even offended the London critics by comparing Tschaikowsky with Beethoven, to Beethoven's disadvantage. And these revivals seem to show, more than anything, Diaghilev's nostalgia for an art that had changed and grown beyond his control. We may suppose that Diaghilev's taste, in Music, Painting and Dancing alike, was really of the simplest, beneath the incrustations of revolutionary snobism; that the pretty, the charming, the melodious and the obviously glamorous pleased him best; that, remaining dominant as a person and implacable as a tyrant, he was, none the less, rather bewildered, as an æsthetic apparatus, by the progressive work he had set progressing, in all directions at once, round about him; that he was puzzled and suspicious of Jean Cocteau's whimsy satire, the quaint noises of Stravinsky, Prokofiev, Erik Satie, the eccentric geometry of

Picasso and the abruptly angular movements which were
the obsession of Massine's choregraphic style, already; and
that he wanted Tschaikowsky's melodies, now, and Petipa's
smooth modulations of structure, mainly because he longed
home-sickly for something he himself could understand and
enjoy. Either way, though, Diaghilev's 1921 Classicism had
to be bigger and better than even Petipa's 1890 Classicism.
Spessivsteva, Trefilova, Egorova, Carlotta Brianza, had to
be fetched from Russia, to be added to Lopokhova, Tchernicheva, Schollar and the rest. There had, in fact, to be
eight ballerine, instead of one. Bakst had to weld Piranesi,
the Bibbienas, the Vienna masques and the Versailles ballets into an ornamental splendour never seen before. Nijinska had to hot up the choregraphy (the Dance of the
Three Ivans, for instance, is hers, not Petipa's). And,
when *La Belle au Bois Dormant* was first shown, in London,
at the Alhambra, it was evidently more an expression of
Diaghilev Enjoying Himself than of the Russian School.

It was, however, the end of Diaghilev's straight commerce with Ballet. The enormous sets took too long
changing, so that the first-night audience and the Press
were bored. In two months, Diaghilev was almost penni-
less. The scenery was detained by his creditors and, by the
next summer, had perished, with all the costumes: except,
that is, one scene, which had to be used, with Alexander
Benois's costumes for *Le Pavillon d'Armide,* to piece together a one-act résumé, *Aurora's Wedding:* this was
immediately welcomed and has stayed in the repertory
ever since. After Massine, Karsavina and Lopokhova left
the company, Bakst fell inconsiderately ill. More scenery
perished, of rain, in a railway siding. The depleted company gathered in Monte Carlo, to wait for its short spring

season there. And Diaghilev's aggrieved line of reasoning must have ended in the thought that, if this was what happened when he tried to give the world Ballet, at its purest, then the responsibility for what followed was the world's. To Hell with Ballet, altogether. . . . Ballet went to Hell, for the next seven years, or to Limbo, anyway, and remained there for some time after. And Composite Diaghilev Theatre took its place, a half-way house for many rarer monsters.

Diaghilev's later productions will have unreckonable significance for the Theatre of the Future, whatever form it takes. That is certain. Some general notions of the Way the Theatre is Going were ventilated in the last chapter, and it is evident, at least, that we are aiming unanimously away from Naturalism now, and towards comprehensive stylisation, in a Theatre that will acknowledge itself to be Theatre, in fact, and not a Slice of Life. In the form that such a Theatre evolves, the key-problems must, I fancy, be musical; for Poetry, Plastic and Histrionics have already been exploited in most of the conceivable non-musical ways; and the Cyclorama, though London managers and producers behave very coyly about it, is capable of almost everything in the way of expressive lighting, while the possibilities of Music, before Diaghilev (and excepting the very doubtful forms of Wagnerian and neo-Wagnerian Music-Drama), had been well-realised only in Italian Opera and Classical Russian Ballet, which are both self-contained forms, hardly capable, as I have argued for Ballet, of assimilation to the Drama. Diaghilev's production of Moussorgsky's *Boris Godounov*, at the Paris Opéra in 1908, was already important, for this is the most satisfying stage-music since Mozart and the first true Music-Drama. But it was Diaghilev's later use of his own musicians which showed us Music as being able to provide a continuum, a medium of interfusion, for almost any range of contradictory parts; and this gives him as great practical importance, in the Theatre, certainly, as can be claimed by Appia, Reinhardt, Stanislavsky, Gordon Craig or any of Diaghilev's superiors in sincerity and intelligence, whose work has been everywhere impeded by their dependence on the commercial enterprise of others.

In this concentration on the possibilities of Music, the Dance was, as I have suggested, increasingly emptied of importance, for Music is the most abstract, as the Dance is the most concrete art, except when the two exist altogether for each other's sake. Some of the great dancers remained, or were replaced by Alexandra Danilova, Felia Doubrouska, Vera Nemtchinova, Alice Nikitina, Anton Dolin, Sergei Lifar, whose personalities, certainly, were displayed to the best advantage. The work of great painters, also, was used; of Picasso, of Matisse. And, to keep pure Ballet warm, there were one or two pieces where Georges Balanchine was allowed to work out a choregraphic lyricism that has once touched the perfection of *Les Sylphides*. But dancers and painters were both subordinate to Diaghilev's vicarious musico-theatrical experiments: were used, along with singers and even acrobats, to make new entertainment-forms for which the various choregraphers, not excepting Bronislawa Nijinska, Nijinsky's sister, who had a very definite creative talent, acted simply as producers and stage-managers. Diaghilev, the director, was supreme, and his best creatures were the music-makers: which does not mean, however, that the music was chiefly interesting, as Music. The main appeal of these ballets was visual and above all, literary, and the music's importance lay in its power to permit these afresh, theatrically, in new permutations and combinations.

The first of Diaghilev's musical analysts was Igor Stravinsky. Let me insist, again, that Stravinsky was the best composer of music for ballets since Tchaikowsky. Though limited in many ways, though working for Diaghilev debauched him and although he was, and is, as I said, congenitally incapable of constructing a sustained melody, or of developing a borrowed one, yet his rhythmic power and his feeling for the Theatre have scarcely been equalled. But he has always been very much the émigré, the cosmopolitan, without racial or cultural roots, and afflicted, in consequence, with an odd spiritual vulgarity which made him the perfect agent for Diaghilev's schemes, whether the schemes themselves were or were not vulgar. After the superb *Firebird* and *Petrouchka,* after *Le Sacre du Printemps* and *Le Chant du Rossignol,* came *Pulcinella,* towards the close of Massine's reign, on which Constant Lambert has written, very happily, that

'Stravinsky was by far the best person for Diaghileff to send time travelling in the eighteenth century because, both temperamentally and racially, he was out of touch with the whole period. A Frenchman or an Italian might have felt some embarrassment about jazzing up the classics, but Stravinsky is like a child delighted with a book of eighteenth-century engravings, yet not so impressed that it has any twinges of conscience about reddening the noses, or adding moustaches and beards in thick black pencil. . . . Yet there is something touchingly naïve about Stravinsky's attitude towards Pergolesi. . . . Like a savage standing in delighted awe before those two symbols of an alien civilisation, the top hat and the pot de chambre, he is apt to confuse their functions.'

Damages

After this, *Renard*, in 1922, *Les Noces*, in 1923, and *Apollo Musagetes*, in 1928. . . . But smart music had moved to Paris, and Diaghilev, to breast ahead of his time, had to give more rein, now, to the Paris school, to the syndicate of Les Six, to François Poulenc and Georges Auric, in particular, to Darius Milhaud, Erik Satie and some hangers-on.

All this musical side of the business, though, can quite well be left to Mr. Lambert, both the accomplished pasticheurs in their own right and the later Diaghilev hacks, Dukelsky, Sauguet, Nabokhov, Rieti and their equals, 'merely the gunmen executing the commands of their Capone, who, like all great gangsters, never touched firearms himself'. Mr. Lambert has written brilliantly about this period, perhaps too brilliantly, sometimes, and perhaps because he was involved with Diaghilev himself, in *Romeo and Juliet,* in 1926. 'Before the war he created a vogue for the Russian ballet, but after the war he merely created a vogue for vogue'—is a little bit too neat, though true enough to be damaging. But the main trend of Mr. Lambert's thesis is that Diagilev disintegrated Music, atomised it, to adapt it to eccentric theatrical purposes. And that, most certainly, is true. It may have hurt Music. The theatrical purposes also may have been misguided. The two important facts are, however, that Diaghilev prosecuted experiments in the Theatre with an energy and a range not equalled elsewhere and that the Art of Dance was not twisted long enough in any one direction to have been materially affected by these experiments.

Each of the twenty-three later Diaghilev ballets was, in fact, a form, was in a kind, of its own, and the main usefulness of the dancers was that they showed themselves to be

far more adaptable, or long-suffering, than any company of
straight actors would ever have been, even under a ruler
like Diaghilev. In *Les Noces,* they rehearsed a peasant marriage, to drums and four pianos, while singers sang about
it. In *Les Fâcheux,* they played Molière in dumb show. In
Les Tentations de la Bergère, Anton Dolin was dressed in
muslin, roses and a blond wig and made indistinguishable
from Lubov Tchernicheva. In *Barabau,* they all had to wear
false noses, padded behinds and bowler hats, which may be
amusing, but do not make a good costume to dance in. *Le
Pas d'Acier* was apparently an attempt to put the Soviet
Film on a stage. *Romeo and Juliet* took place back-stage, in
Pirandello fashion. *Ode* was a piece designed to exploit the
Cinematograph, cyclorama-wise, and the geometric possibilities of rope. Sergei Lifar's revision of *Renard* used
trained acrobats, and the dancers were made to imitate
their antics.

And so on. . . . They were all interesting experiments, if
rather hysterical and rather unkind to the dancers. This
last eccentricity, of *Renard,* derived from Dolin's acrobatics
in *Le Train Bleu.* Here, as testimony to the general argument, is Diaghilev's own preface to the London production of that ballet.

'*The first point about "Le Train Bleu" is that there is no blue
train in it. This being the age of speed, it has already reached its
destination and disembarked its passengers. These are to be seen
on a beach which does not exist, in front of a casino which exists
still less. Overhead passes an aeroplane which you do not see, and
the plot represents nothing. And yet when it was presented for the
first time in Paris everybody was unaccountably seized with the
desire to take the blue train to Deauville and perform refreshing
exercises. Moreover, this ballet is not a ballet. It is an opérette*

Damages

dansée. *The music is by Darius Milhaud, but it has nothing in common with the music that we associate with Darius Milhaud. It is danced by the real Russian ballet, but it has nothing to do with Russian ballet. It was invented for Anton Dolin, a classical dancer who does nothing classical. The scenery is painted by a sculptor and the costumes are by a great arbiter of fashion who has never made a costume.'*

It must have been all very trying. But here, for reference, is the full tale of Diaghilev ballets, excepting the classical revivals and leaving quite apart the ballets by Fokine and Massine (in this period, *Cimarosiana, Les Matelots, Zephyr and Flora, Las Meninas, Le Pas d'Acier, Mercure* and *Ode*).

BOOK	MUSIC	COSTUMES AND SETTINGS	CHOREGRAPHY
		1912	
		L'Après-Midi d'un Faune	
Mallarmé	Debussy	Bakst	Nijinsky
		1913	
		Le Sacre du Printemps	
Roerich	Stravinsky	Roerich	Nijinsky
		Jeux	
Nijinsky	Debussy	Bakst	Nijinsky
		La Tragédie de Salome	
Romanov	Schmitt	Soudeikine	Romanov
		1921	
		Choût	
Larionov	Prokofiev	Larionov	Larionov
		1922	
		Renard	
Stravinsky	Stravinsky	Larionov	Nijinska (Lifar, 1929)
		1923	
		Les Noces	
Stravinsky	Stravinsky	Gontscharova	Nijinska

Sergei Pavlovitch Diaghilev and the Aftermath

BOOK	MUSIC	COSTUMES AND SETTINGS	CHOREGRAPHY
		1924	
		Les Biches	
	Poulenc	Laurencin	Nijinska
		Les Fâcheux	
Molière-Kochno	Auric	Braque	Nijinska (Massine, 1927)
		Les Tentations de la Bergère	
	Montéclair-Casadesus	Gris	Nijinska
		Le Train Bleu	
Cocteau	Milhaud	Chanel-Laurens-Picasso	Nijinska
		1925	
		Barabau	
Rieti	Rieti	Utrillo	Balanchine (De Valois, 1936)
		La Pastorale	
Kochno	Auric	Pruna	Balanchine
		1926	
		Jack-in-the-Box	
	Satie-Milhaud	Dérain	Balanchine
		Romeo and Juliet	
	Lambert	Ernst-Miró	Nijinska
		1927	
		La Chatte	
Aesop-Sobeka	Sauguet	Gabo-Pevsner	Balanchine
		1928	
		Apollo Musagetes	
	Stravinsky	Bauchant	Balanchine
		The Gods go a-Begging	
	Handel-Beecham	Bakst-Gris	Balanchine (De Valois, 1936)

Damages

BOOK	MUSIC	COSTUMES AND SETTINGS	CHOREGRAPHY

1929
The Prodigal Son

Kochno	Prokofiev	Rouault	Balanchine

Le Bal

Kochno	Rieti	Chirico	Balanchine

Details of all these later productions are available in W. A. Propert's too adulatory but well-written and beautifully illustrated book on the period, to which I owe a good deal myself, while Arnold L. Haskell's definitive biography (which would carefully combat every general assertion I have made) must be known to almost all my readers.

Resuming, then, and coming to the Aftermath. . . . Diaghilev's achievement was an achievement for the Theatre, as a whole, and his influence on Ballet was circumstantial, not direct. That is to say, he effected no change in the Art of Dance, but he effected a great many experimental changes in the conditions under which the Art of Dance is presented. In the slaking of his own colossal Will to Power, in drawing together as many arts, as many means as possible of entangling the world's emotions, into one giant engine of domination, he produced a range of tentative new Theatre-forms which, though chaotic and largely accidental, will give him great significance for the Theatre of the Future, whatever shape it may take. But it was the accident of his early work in the Russian Imperial Theatres which made Ballet dancers come to be

the stock creatures of his Theatre rather than Opera singers, acrobats, free dancers or plain actors, though he used
all these, too. His dancers were produced by Cecchetti and
the Russian School and owed nothing to him as dancers.
Their work, in fact, was smothered, though its appeals and
glamours were heightened, by the far more obtrusive work
of the loudest and funniest painters and musicians. And
there was never enough homogeneity or continuity for any
Style Diaghilev to be evolved in Choregraphy. The greatest
Diaghilev choregrapher, Michel Fokine, was matured before the Diaghilev Company was born, and Léonide Massine, though in many ways his mind was of Diaghilev's formation, has increased its stature since his death, while
Georges Balanchine's master-work, *Cotillon,* dates back
only to 1933.

The important matter, in fact, is whether the circumstantial effects of Diaghilev's career, both on Ballet itself
and on the surrounding fields, have been good or bad. And
they ought to have been good. It was in the nature of the
lessons he gave to teach what needed teaching. If they have
not produced their due effect, it was not Diaghilev's fault.
In the first place, it may be important that he got Ballet out
of Russia before the Revolution, though he was much
tempted by Lenin's offer to take it back, after the Revolution. Either way, his own basic achievement, viewed socio-
logically, was spadework for Ballet as a Democratic Art,
and this despite the fact that he was himself the supreme
individualist, the most terrific Imperial-Monopolist in Art
there has ever been. He took the Russian School's dancers
out of their concentration camp, their apparent position as
an Imperial-Court harem with male-dancer guardians, and
set them in fresh, in hectic contact with all the artistic and

social turbulence of pre-war, war-time and post-war Western Europe. Though he overlaid the structure of Ballet with every kind of weighty irrelevance, yet he left the essential forms of Ballet untouched. And the clearest showing of his many synthetic structures was a very salutary and, potentially, supremely helpful showing of many of the kinds of matters that Ballet cannot assimilate. Many people, here and there, in Western Europe, must have got beneath the masking overlay and taken essential Ballet to themselves (despite the failure of *La Belle au Bois Dormant*) for the first time. And Diaghilev as a disruptive force most certainly disrupted the right things. He drew to a focus—blew one enormous bubble out of—nearly everything that was dreadful in the intellectual and spiritual life of his day, and this enormous bubble exploded, like Oscar Wilde, with his death, leaving little of its composition but a few hundred bewildered and forgotten æsthetes, dribbling helplessly about the places of their former glory and dreaming of the vanished days.

As to the dancers themselves, and the choreographers, whom Diaghilev had uprooted out of Russia. . . . Their dispersion, at his death, cannot have harmed them, and it has done the world a world of good. Diaghilev's best dancers, for the most part, and some of the lesser ones, either founded schools of their own or went off to work in Cabaret. Both of which were excellent things to do. . . . Cabaret work may vulgarise, but it does bring in new audiences for Ballet, and it does draw out some of the best qualities of the Dance. Though stylistically very simple and obvious, the Can-Can, for instance, technically, is almost pure Ballet. To dance it, in front of the audiences for whom it is danced, sets the Dancer in such a relation to essential aspects of the

age as must inevitably be fruitful of specifically modern stylistic forms. And some of the finest contemporary dancers
owe much of their personal excellence to a spell of work
in Cabaret. What is still more important, though, is that
the schools, now scattered over wide areas, have brought
the Art of Dance to a very high level in nearly every country. Fokine and Balanchine, Koslov and Mordkine, in
America. . . . They have not yet been endowed with permanent theatres to work in, but they can do much to con-
tracept such very American births as Ted Shawn and his
Ensemble of Men Dancers. In Paris, Olga Spessivtseva,
Vera Trefilova, Sergei Lifar, with the two supreme teachers, Kchessinskaya and Preobrajenskaia. . . . In this country
(after Astafieva, Enrico Cecchetti himself, and with Nicolas
Legat, still, to provide a focus in the older traditions),
Sokolova and Idzikowsky and now, supremely, Marie
Rambert and Ninette de Valois.

Permanent companies soon began to form, too, none of
them so vast in single scope as Diaghilev's, but operating,
altogether, over a much vaster field. In Russia, the old intensive training from the cradle is no longer possible, but
the work done there now, has more true relation to the
whole community than was ever possible before. The
Revolution left such fine dancers as Gueltzer and Volkova
for the old ballets (*Le Lac des Cygnes* is still, it seems, the
general favourite), while Semenova, entirely a child of
the Revolution, is thought, by some discerning judges, to
have no equal in Western Europe. And the Communists
have definite educational schemes in connection with Ballet. We had some very amusing accounts of these, recently,
from Igor Schwezov, but there is at least this much positive value in them: they show that the U.S.S.R. has not

fallen into the easy fallacy of believing that the way to re-store the Dance to its fullest place in the community is to make it so easy that everybody can do it, which is what Isadora was after. Elsewhere. . . . Nemtchinova, with Nicolas Zverev and Anatol Oboukhov, went off to Kovno and have shown us, since, the National Ballet of Lithuania, which has not only permitted Vera Nemtchinova herself to become a very great artist indeed, but has drawn into Ballet with her, a charming young race and a temperament new to us. Hungary, also, has channelled its national glamour and frenzy into Ballet's forms. Ballet is preserved, at its old height, in Milan, Vienna, Warsaw, all the old capitals, and has grown up in most of the younger ones, like Bel-grade.

The first important English Ballet was the Camargo Society, which Edwin Evans, Arnold L. Haskell and P. J. S. Richardson gave us, in 1927. Their work was taken over and strengthened, five years later, in the Vic-Wells Ballet, under Ninette de Valois, which has shown us, in Alicia Markova, an English dancer quite incomparable. Mme. Rambert's school was given a sharp focus in 1931, by the acquisition of a small private theatre, the Mercury, over which, most appropriately, stands a gilded reproduction of Boulogne's figure, en attitude, and which, in the person of Ashley Dukes, fosters, equally, the little work that is being done in London for Poetic Drama. And, here, apart from Mme. Rambert's superb teaching work, which has given us, already, some very fine dancers, one young choregrapher has matured whose work, I suspect, may come to be the most important choregraphic work of our day, though his output, as yet, is small, his scope being so limited. And then, after some tentative mixing of seasons of Ballet and Opera,

Sergei Pavlovitch Diaghilev and the Aftermath

Colonel W. de Basil formed his Ballets Russes de Monte Carlo, with Léonide Massine as Master and Choregrapher; with Lubov Tchernicheva and Sergei Grigoriev, her husband, for the school and production; with Alexandra Danilova for prima ballerina and with a big company of young dancers (including, for the 1935 season, five English members, five Americans, one Dane, one German and one Japanese),[8] among whom, though stylistically unformed still, there are some miracles of technical accomplishment. They brought Ballet back to London, to the Alhambra, an old home of Ballet, on July 4th, 1933, with all Diaghilev's old fire, and it seemed true, as Mr. Haskell has it, in his Preface to the 1935 season, that

'These children showed us a technique unknown to their famous elders; with them 32 fouettés entered into the normal repertoire and were no more a flashy trick. . . . These dancers are in the most direct line of tradition; artistic children of Preobrajenska, Kchessinskaya, Egorova, Trefilova and Volinine, and they are daily adding to tradition.'

---

[8] The Japanese lady keeps her own name, Sono Osato, which is exotic enough, for Western ears, to mix with the rest. The others have variously changed their names. Three of the English members for instance, whose names were once Betty Cuff, Prudence Hyman and Elizabeth Ruxton (all pupils of Mme. Rambert's), were strangely transformed into Vera Nelidova, Paulina Strogova and Lisa Serova. This Russianising of the names of dancers is a nice problem. It is less of a snobism, I think, than it was, and in a predominantly Russian company, it does make for the virtue of Impersonality. But there is a faint unpleasantness about it, all the same, for those who find that a name is a pleasant and significant thing: besides which it leads the dancers into cultivating quite alien Russian mannerisms, and this, apart from being a supreme affectation, militates against any achievement of a national stylistic integrity. English Ballet, certainly, has been harmed by it. Perhaps, eventually, we shall come to the use of numerals?

Damages

True, or almost true. . . . Technical values which have established themselves, like Man's erect stature and the giraffe's neck. . . . And, if prosperity matters, there ought to be no limit to our jubilation. The London Ballet Season has, in effect, been abolished. We now have Ballet all the year round. A sorting out of last year's programmes, for instance, reveals no more than a fortnight's break, in August. In February, the Rambert Ballet (which had been giving weekly performances since the previous October) had a West End season, at the Duke of York's. In March, the National Ballet of Lithuania showed us the mature Nemtchinova, for a month, at that oldest home of Ballet, the Alhambra. In May, the Vic-Wells Ballet (which, also, had been dancing continuously since the previous October) took on a special season at Sadler's Wells, with an extension into Shaftesbury Avenue (of all places), and then—most important happening of all—took Classical Ballet, with Markova and Dolin, out into the Provinces. The de Basil Company had Covent Garden from June 11th to August 24th. Les Ballets Russes de Paris—Stanislas Idzikowsky—attempted a fortnight's competition and then went off to Golder's Green. At the beginning of September, we had the first view of what seemed a most exciting new company, Les Ballets Russes de Léon Woizikowsky, with Ruth Chanova and André Eglevsky, who, though a mere boy still, is probably the purest classical dancer we have. And, by the time his season ended, not only were our two resident companies both at work again—and that with

Plate 6. Tamara Toumanova in her dressing-room at Covent Garden (made up for *L'Oiseau de Feu*). *Howard Coster Photograph.*

twice as many performances as before—but there had also occurred a phenomenon called the British Ballet, which concluded its performances with profane hymns to an enormous gilded Britannia and, for anything I know (for I was unhappily out of London), Lady Houston coming down on a wire.

All this, too, was interrupted by numerous incursions of non-Ballet and anti-Ballet, from Antonia Mercé and the Javanese Prince Raden Mas Jodjana to Ted Shawn and his Ensemble of Men Dancers or Alanova and her Assortment of Expensive Dresses. The thoroughly admirable International Institute of Margaret Morris Movement held a whole week's demonstrations of work which, apart from anything else, has important bearings on Obstetrics, Britain's Failure to Win the Olympic Games and the Cause and Cure of Constipation. The first International Folk Dance Festival was held in London, in July, with a tremendous show of national forms that Ballet still has to exploit. And the highest-browed of all our periodicals, in the course of its quarterly Dying for the Flag about Culture and A Truly Contemporary Sensibility, announced, in March, that

'There is much to be said for regarding ballet, at the present time, as an art form of considerable importance.'

It seems, in fact, as if—at the very least—Ballet had found out, fully and finally, what she was after, and we were all getting on, untroubled, with the job in hand. But it isn't so. It was never less so. Throughout the whole amazing season, very little new work of importance was produced. Massine's two new ballets were as thoroughly muddled as anything he or anybody else has ever given us. There never has been so much technically brilliant dancing in the world, nor so many theatres open to dancing. But Ballet no more knows what she is up to than Literature does, or Music, or Painting. It is a good moment for some form of Ballet Criticism to arise.

This is not a kind of sarcasm or irony. Nor is it a special plea on behalf of this book. There has been no need for serious Criticism, in Ballet, until just now. From 1681, when Ballet left the Court and Mlle. Lafontaine was installed in History as the first true ballerina, the problem of Ballet was single and remained so to the end of the nineteenth century: to extend technical powers and evolve a coherent Style that should embody, to the fullest possible extent, all the qualities of sharpness and breadth, clarity of outline and swift progression that delineate Western Culture as a whole. The problem was not solved until Cecchetti had taken the Italian acrobatic power to Russia, to be refined and consolidated, in the hot-house Imperial Schools, by Johanssen, Petipa and Nicolas Legat. Critical standards (as distinct from pedagogic standards) would, in such a process, have been irrelevant. Noverre, as I said, was an anachronism. There was no need for critical standards, even, when the Diaghilev Company, taking Ballet out again into the great wide world, was trying out all the ways in which the evolved coherent Style might be applied. For this phase, popular technical exposition was required, because Ballet was becoming a democratic art, and that need was supplied by such as Valerian Svetlov and André Levinson. Gossip and general personal information, also, such as Mr. Haskell still so painstakingly supplies, had their legitimate place, in exciting and focusing interest. But Ballet Criticism, meaning a similar thing to Literary Criticism, was not necessary until it became quite obvious, last year or the year before, that, with all the accumulation of new forces, the substantial lessons of Diaghilev's career of instruction had simply not been learnt.

B. New Perspectives

Lessons, mostly, after Fokine's departure from the company, in what matters Ballet cannot handle. . . . To formulate those lessons is the first and main task of Ballet Criticism, now. To learn them is the main immediate task of Ballet. And the basic one is that T. S. Eliot was substantially wrong when he wrote, in 1926, that

'The ballet will probably be one of the influences forming a new drama, if a new drama ever comes. I mean, of course, the later ballet.'

This is reïteration, but it is necessary. Ballet is not expressive, in literary senses. By its nature, it expresses only itself, which is to say, certain general qualities of style. It cannot bear nearly so much weight of dramatic content as any of the more highly developed forms of Free Dancing. Its concern is, first and last, with movement, muscular progression and the abstractedly plastic interplay of human bodies. Ballet is the art of Pure Muscular Style. Its basic material is pure muscular impulses, not ideas, verbal or otherwise. It cannot offer as much material for a future dramatic technique, therefore, as the free experiments of, say, Kurt Jooss, though histrionics will probably owe most, in the future, to the work, at present repressed and submerged, of small groups like Margaret Barr's Dance-Drama Group, which has the good sense to understand that, for such ends, the exploitation of pure theatrical technique is of far greater importance than the evolution of dance-forms.

Diaghilev proved all this, through and through. He tried to do, with Ballet, every conceivable thing that cannot be done with Ballet. In the process, he produced a vast and chaotic range of theatre-forms that any possible Theatre of the Future will owe a vast and chaotic debt to. And Ballet crept out at the corner, every time. As far as Ballet is concerned, these monsters lie slain in their own lymph, once and for all. They are colossal stuffed warnings. They are like the stuffed sabre-toothed tigers and mastodons of South Kensington: horrible warnings of what happens when Nature is too ambitious. And their main teaching is, now, that, in any composite theatrical art of the future, Ballet must stand apart. Or else it will be abandoned. If it insists on blowing itself out to mastodon size, Ballet, also, will stand, one day, with ponderous stuffed gravity, in a museum. We have not understood Diaghilev. We have not appreciated him, for, if we had, we should understand that the best tribute to him would be to acknowledge our debt and 'do otherwise'. Instead of which, we still suck energy from his corpse and feebly imitate. . . . We still experiment, aimlessly, feebly, and not in stylistic ways, but in the way of incorporating more and more discursive, more dramatic, more literary elements into Ballet. 'These things . . . have not tainted down to its substantial self. . . . The organic central tradition persists. . . . Ballet cannot become inwrenched . . . without ceasing to be Ballet . . .' But we try to make Ballet fulfil the functions which present-day Drama is not fulfilling, and because, in Drama, some degree of Naturalism is needed, not Pure Style, most of our experiments could use the manners of the forms of Free Dancing equally well—better—and could dispense with even the technique of Ballet.

Altogether. . . . A technical regression beyond Cecchetti is not inconceivable. Since Fokine, there is no created body of work, anywhere, though there are a good many isolated pieces, which can be held to extend organically the Classical Tradition, much less to show authoritatively what direction Ballet can now take. Our choregraphers, everywhere, are 'playing into the hands' of Central Europe and the multitudinous progeny of Isadora Duncan. This is the main aspect of the present situation, after Massine's *Les Présages, Choreartium* and *Union Pacific.* Meanwhile, as I said in my first chapter, 'intellectually, a gathering of the pundits of Ballet'—who might be expected to draw up standards, maintain values, check the course of Ballet and provide, at least, intellectual coherence and continuity—'is not clearly distinguishable from, say, the deliberations of a poultry-fanciers' association.' There is too much Literary Criticism, but Ballet Criticism is wanted, to keep Ballet from getting lost in the unlimited mass of material theoretically at her disposal. There is a good deal of truth in an aphorism of Samuel Butler's.

'*The youth of an art is, like the youth of anything else, its most interesting period. When it has come to the knowledge of good and evil, it is stronger, but we care less for it.*'
Ballet, however, still in its youth as a pure art, has become involved, helplessly, in the general good and evil of the world in which it subsists, and it has to understand and take account of its situation, now, or it will go roaring to perdition with the other arts, the knowing ones, the hags.

The first serious piece of English Ballet Criticism was published the year before last, and, much as I, for one, liked it, I think it was an unfortunate beginning. Adrian Stokes's is a brilliant and impressive mind. That, I think, should be clear from what passages of his I have quoted. But he has, as it seems to me, too much capacity for enjoyment, especially for visual enjoyment. The consequence is that, while he illuminates certain aspects of Ballet in an altogether exquisite way, he has not, in my opinion, been successful in organising his illuminations with a corresponding critical zest. I cannot agree with the common—the dancers'—objections to Mr. Stokes's writings, that he 'always sees more in Ballet than there ever was'. It can be said of works of art in general that they always contain at least the sum of what all the intelligent people in the world can see in them, that what the artist consciously put there is never more than a minute fraction of the total significance. But Mr. Stokes sees exclusively. He is altogether absorbed in the pleasures of seeing. His appreciation is too purely visual. He makes no assumption, therefore, and comes to no conclusion, to distinguish Ballet, at all fundamentally, from, say, the Silly Symphonies of Walt Disney. The distinctive feature of dancing—that its primary material is a muscular apparatus, not a coloured shape, a noise or a general idea—is pointed out, several times, and then, in practice, ignored. The Dance, for Mr. Stokes, is a visual art. It is pictures brought to life. And when, as it must, the art of the colour-symphony (foreshadowed, for instance, by such experimenters as, in this country, Len Lye) is brought to a condition in which it has to be considered seriously, all Mr. Stokes's critical principles, for the Dance, may be found to be irrelevant.

In the meantime, however, they are principles on which the minds of a good many enthusiasts—and critics and, worst of all, choreographers—seem to work. And I believe them to be dangerous to Ballet. Dangerous in themselves, they become more so by the fact that they mix very easily with other dangerous principles, with the principles of literary expressiveness, for instance. Mr. Stokes himself has denounced dancing which wants to be expressive in literary ways. Some of his best passages are made up of such denunciation. Nevertheless, he has found it necessary to pack all the ballets he writes about with a very full literary content, no less irrelevant for being and acknowledging itself to be private and inessential. His second book is, I think, not as good as the first; but it is thoroughly pertinent and quite fair to note, here, that, in this second book, though the author still needs to visualise even the music before he can come to terms with it, yet his slippery material and his initial approach to it, an initial refusal, as I see it, to assess dancing in its own essential terms, of muscular impact, have so far forced him into the use of literary standards and the abrogation of the original plastic sensibility as to let him praise *Les Présages* highly, decor and all, indeed to let him use *Les Présages,* with the later *Choreartium,* as a point of reference for all Ballet. 'It would, perhaps, be true to say that I have written throughout in the light of . . .' Which means that Mr. Stokes, while continuing faithful to the Classical Tradition, has endorsed Massine's complete and final regression from it.

Massine himself, however, is more important than prose-poems written in his name. And the clearest facts about Massine, as choreographer, are that he worked always on the basis of what was once called character dancing (in particular, the stylised Spanish Dance of Petipa, zapateado, up-thrusting arms and all, and the temps levés of the

Damages

Czardas); that, consciously, he was never, in fact, fundamentally concerned at all, to develop the Classical Tradition; and that he appears, at the moment, to have exhausted the available forces in his own line. The trouble
set in, finally, with *Les Présages*. And it was inevitable, I
fancy, as soon as the music was chosen. Tschaikowsky's
Fifth Symphony is at the opposite extreme to the music
Tschaikowsky wrote for Ballet. In itself it is literary: it demands, from the Dancer, interpretation, not dancing. It is
not self-contained music. No serious purist objection can
be urged against its use for non-musical purposes. But the
movements it calls for are dramatic movements, elaborate
energetic mime, the sort of technique that Kurt Jooss has
evolved, in sublime unity of purpose, in this, with Isadora
Duncan, Valeska Gert and the daisy-picking schools in
general. Massine, of course, has not lost control of his
material, not yet. He is the only living choreographer who
could have borne up at all, beneath all this weight of Literature. And I imagine, though I have not seen it in rehearsal,
that *Les Présages* must be an enjoyable piece of work, a fine
vigorous structure, done in practice dress.

But the cosmic setting, with its comets and pulsating
curves and colorific reminiscence of blood, pus and cam-
phorated oil. . . . The boys and girls of the chorus pre-
tending to be something between Spartan warriors and
proletarians of the New Dawn. . . . Above all, Jasinsky,
done up as a bunch of blighted and galvanised sage, to represent Fate. . . . This is not only Literature. It is Bad Literature. What followed it—*Choreartium*—has none of the simple dreadfulness of *Les Présages*. It is Dalcrozian interpretation of music, rather than a choreographic structure. It derives too much of its effect from the music. Its use of

masses is a bad, a non-balletic, a tableaux-vivants use. For me, at any rate, it has finally killed Brahms's Fourth Symphony: sucking up all Brahms's restless energy into visual and muscular forms (which seem, then, as if the energy were natively and properly theirs) and leaving the music itself, for single consumption, drained and ineffective. *Choreartium,* in fact, is everything (with its trailingly mysterious Central European second movement, its spring songs, monastery gardens, Nietzschean heroes and Heinean women) that one must disapprove of, as tendency, at least. But it does contrive to be satisfying in a way that very few ballets are. The perfect theatrical exploitation of two very rich personalities—the miraculously expressive arms of Nina Verchinina and the strange compound of heroic strength and almost feminine softness that is David Lichine —in itself makes any performance supremely enjoyable. The poetic imagery which Massine has used is so very confused that it is possible, on a fourth or fifth seeing, to put the bad Literature out of one's head entirely and contemplate the work as pure Choregraphy. The unusual use of compounded doubles tours, in the last movement, is one of the most overpowering effects of choreographic virtuosity in the whole of Ballet. And it did indeed seem, when *Choreartium* was first let loose on us, that a very great clarification was preparing, and that Massine was paving, with these bad intentions, the road to some quite inconceivable choregraphic heaven.

He wasn't. He was getting ready to give us *Union Pacific.* The Cosmos had exhausted him, and he was going to play to the gallery as no choregrapher had ever dared to do. Someone had to do it, eventually, I suppose. But, apart from the disappointment in Massine, that the libretto

should proceed from so good a poet as Archibald Mac-
Leish was one cause for wonder and dismay. That the lovely
Irina Baronova (who had almost saved even *Les Présages*
from futility) should have to coax the disciplined richness
of her grace into a bad imitation of Jessie Matthews was
another. And it was a cause for dismay, if no longer for
wonder, that an English audience should applaud with such
indiscriminate generosity. What was to come had already
looked bad enough, from the preliminary announcements.
'*Union Pacific:* An American Ballet in One Act and Four
Scenes, Libretto by Archibald MacLeish, Music by Nicolas
Nabokoff based on folk songs of the period 1860, Choreography by Léonide Massine, etc. . . .' Ballet with words
had been hinted at, though the knowing ones (for me, at
that time, 'the lads in the orchestra') had said nothing.
Carl Sandburg came to mind. The music caption invoked
Stephen Leacock. On the whole, something in the way of
Soviet Expressionism was to be expected, transplanted and
naturalised, and something of that sentimental love of
power-houses and smokestacks and childlike curiosity about
cog-wheels which still account for so much of the imagery
of modern verse (and music and painting), shielding itself
from adult reprobation with a gauzy veil of 'satirical intent'.

But that was nothing to the reality. First, Eglevsky, who
'danced the attributes' of steam and pistons, in front of a
blue print, and who was evidently much embarrassed by not
being allowed to chuff and whistle. . . . Tender-making
laughterous ingenuity of Irish workmen, who laid down

Plate 7. *Choriatium:* Fourth Movement. Decor. by C.
Terechkovitch and E. Lourié. *Malcolm Dunbar Photograph,*

human rails and proceeded to use their arms as spanners and tap-hammers. . . . Petrov, in white buckskin (Petrov, the finest of all supporters in the classical Adagio), and a rival gang of Chinese: to whom enters the Lady Gay, Baronova (poor girl), doing Mae West, rather badly. . . . Thence to the Big Tent, notorious saloon. . . . Dance of Mexicans, Dance of Gamblers: both very Russian. . . . The high spot: Massine shuffling and wriggling with such zest and rhythmical precision and so exciting the gallery that he had to do an encore (and, I suppose, pay a fine for it, afterwards). . . . So on, till the Irish and the Chinese come to blows, in a choreographic rough house that looks exactly like a game of musical chairs. . . . And then the last scene, which, being indescribable, let the programme describe . . .

'*The scene shifts back to the road-bed of the line. The hostility of the Big Tent has become a rivalry in work. The two gangs, driving the rails before them, approach each other, while cheering crowds of women and Indians and Mexicans look on. The last rail is about to be laid. Pompously and solemnly the capitalists enter. The golden spike is driven into the tie of laurel. The telegraph instrument beside the track ticks out the word D-O-N-E. And while the nation celebrates with cannon and bells in San Francisco and Omaha and Chicago, and with the hymn "Old Hundred", played upon Trinity chimes in New York, the capitalists and workmen and girls and Indians pose before the camera at Promotory Point.*'

But indescribable, as it actually happened. . . . Choreographic form demanding balance and repetition, the rival gangs met, twice, in the centre of the stage. Then chaos was come again, though a vague sense persists of cardboard locomotives and several white-haired Lincolns from plays in some provincial Temperance Hall, with a feeling of

Damages

The Firebird's last-act superbity being finally reduced to the absurd. And thousands of thumping palms wafted up the conviction, to one not yet in the way of grace, that sylphs and swans, perhaps, were not so bad, after all, and the wish that he'd gone to the Windmill, instead, where they do this sort of thing so much better and with so much less depressing music and with an audience that doesn't think it's absorbing the latest thing in Cosmopolitan Culture.

And that, so far as one can see (it was only two years ago), was the end of Léonide Massine. *Union Pacific* could, conceivably, have been a mere lapse, even after the cosmos-probing of *Les Présages* and *Choreartium*. But last year's re-vision of *Le Bal* (first done by Balanchine as the last of the Diaghilev ballets) and, even more, *Jardin Publique,* suggests that Massine is no longer goaded by any other wish than the wish to be original, and that wearily. *Le Bal* still had some beautiful Adagio movements in it. So had *Union Pacific.* They might have left room for the thought that Massine was working towards a new purpose—the hope is still possible—and that his evident discomfort was a kind of travail. But *Jardin Publique* was tiresome throughout. The most noticeably bad entrée in *Le Bal* was the Spanish entrée, a piece of alternately syncopated and end-stopped creaking angularity that could never have been expected from the choregrapher of *Le Tricorne;* and *Jardin Publique* was most noticeably bad in the Rumba, a possible counterpart to the single thoroughly clever thing (the Barman's Dance) in *Union Pacific.* It is very sad. Yet to acknowledge the implacable fact, if uncharitable, is antiseptic. There may be a resurrection. I hope so, profoundly. And Léonide Massine did mark an epoch. I suggested a term for it. I suggested 'sentimental satire'. Probably all satire is sentimental. Certainly it is in Ballet. For—whatever the libretto may want to have a go at—satirical dancing can only satirise an achieved style, and any style sufficiently achieved to be worth satirising is always worth more than the state of mind of the individual man who wants to satirise it. It is more vigorous, for one thing. A tongue in the cheek is always an impediment, in the expressive arts. But that's nothing to the effect a wooden leg has on a dancer's technique. Massine was having his go (by way of Fokine) at Petipa, at the highest development of pure classical dancing. He was bound to do it wrily. His dominant feeling was bound to be a nostalgia.

Massine's ultimate place in Tradition (both as Diaghilev's most characteristic creature and in his own subsequent right) will be seen, in fact, (unless, now, there is a great reversal), to be that of a short-lived heresy and a heresy prosecuted without much conviction: a sort of rebellious-schoolboy heresy, very attractive and not very powerful. He is the counterpart—so—of the devout and cheerful Michel Fokine. He is self-consciously wicked and rather sad about it. In his best ballets, he was putting his tongue out at *Les Sylphides,* which, however, was much too happy, and had far too much poise, to mind. *Les Sylphides,* of course, is the one quite flawless ballet. It is the one ballet in the repertory that can be enjoyed in a bad performance, for the sheer joy of its logic, its unfolding of choreographic forms. I fancy that most people will agree with me, here. Perhaps for the first time. . . . Yet to acknowledge the supreme excellence of *Les Sylphides* is to acknowledge the pertinence of all the critical values I have asserted. There is no literary content in the ballet, unless it be a vague 'period' flavour (which, in any case, is not specifically literary) and the moon-struck fickleness of mood. *Les Sylphides* is Pure Style. It is the perfect choregraphic interplay of all the main forms that had been in steady process of evolution for several centuries. And it is nothing more, in its own nature. There is no allegiance paid, in it, to anything but Tradition. Its forms unfold to music which, though perfectly worked into the whole organic structure, perfectly chosen, is, in itself, of no importance at all or almost none: while the scenic elements, even when the decors keep closest to Corot (and unless we are giving a coating of tinfoil or too much green in the lighting), are never interesting enough even to be resented. And it is as the immediate rebellion against this kind of perfection (which, in itself, certainly, was not very fruitful for the future, except as a pattern) that Massine's work is chiefly significant.

Massine's best ballet, it seems to me, is *Les Matelots*. *Le Tricorne,* which comes closest to it in excellence, is, though dramatically perfect, choreographically blurred, as a single whole. Its excellences are excellences of detail. I don't suppose everybody will agree with me in this. But even the adorers of *Les Présages* and *Choreartium* will, more often

---

Plate 8. *Les Sylphides*. Toumanova and Paul Petroff. The non-balletomane may care to compare this with the *Jardin aux Lilas* (Plate 12). Mlle. Svetlova in that, Mlle. Toumanova in this, are extended in an arabesque, the posture above all others in which the classical danseuse reveals the perfection or imperfection of her line. *Malcolm Dunbar Photograph.*

New Perspectives

than not, grant *Les Matelots* and *Le Tricorne* next place, unless, perhaps, they go for *La Boutique Fantasque,* with its infinity of mixed and irrelevant brilliances and pathos, or the
remarkable decorative unity which Miró has imposed on
Jeux d'Enfants. At any rate, the point I wish to make is the
seemingly paradoxical point that the excellence of *Les
Matelots* and *Le Tricorne* is entirely classical, though classical
in reverse. It is derived, entirely, from reference to the
Classical Tradition: satirical reference. Not satire in any
literary sense, but pure choregraphic satire. . . . This is evident enough in *Les Matelots.* Auric's music, now that the
fashion he represented has passed, never troubles anybody,
one way or the other. And Pedro Pruna's costumes and
settings, though they are among the best that Ballet has, are
completely non-obtrusive in performance. Those who have
seen the ballet at all will not need reminding of the mock-
classical pas seul of the third sailor or, for that matter, the
straightforward Classicism implicit in the movements of
the (dramatically) quite irrelevant street-musician. And
that, though the ballet unfolds a story, has a literary content, is the whole theme and substance. The spoons-player
—if only by reason of his complete irrelevance to the story
—provides a constant point of reference and a tether: as it
were the Classical Tradition in person, fixed there, vigi-
lant. And every movement takes its significance from that
juxtaposition. Every movement is a more or less directly
satirical comment on the Classical Tradition, in the person of that quite irrelevant dancer,[9] from the exuberant
deftnesses and grotesqueries of the sailors to the senti-

---

[9] His original was an actual griddler, who played the spoons, mag-
nificently, outside the Coliseum, in 1925.

mental vaguenesses of the heroine and the bumpkin awk-
wardness of the servant girl, who presents us with an image
of the human body in its natural state, untouched by any
tradition of the Dance. This is the structure of the work.
This gives it its fine coherence and wry beauty. And, in
that, it depends on the ideal of the Dance as Pure Style,
every bit as much as *Les Sylphides,* though in reverse. It is safe
to say, at any rate, that *Les Matelots* would be lost on anyone
who had never seen a classical ballet. Choreographically, it
would be meaningless.

Whether or not Massine was, or is, aware of all this, of
course, is irrelevant. No creative artist, let me say again,
was ever conscious of more than a small fraction of the
substance of his work. The creative situation uses him, as
an instrument, very often a blind instrument. It is Tradition
goading him, with or without his consent. And it is only
when the operations of Tradition are choked that the
artist has to be highly conscious of what he is up to.

Similar things are true of *Le Tricorne*. Impressive as Picasso and de Falla are, in combination, and beautifully set
out as the story is: from the third or fourth seeing, the
interest centres almost wholly in two or three pieces of
solo and duetto dancing, by the Miller and his wife (the
use of the corps is poor, even by Massine's own tableaux-
vivants standards). And this dancing has at least as much
Classical Ballet in it as of true Spanish dancing. Its basis is
not anything danced in Spain. It is the Spanish Dance of
Petipa. I fancy anyone brought up on Jota, Bolero, Aragon-
ese, would be rather bored by *Le Tricorne*. He would see it

Plate 9. *Le Tricorne.* Léonide Massine. *Malcolm Dunbar
Photograph.*

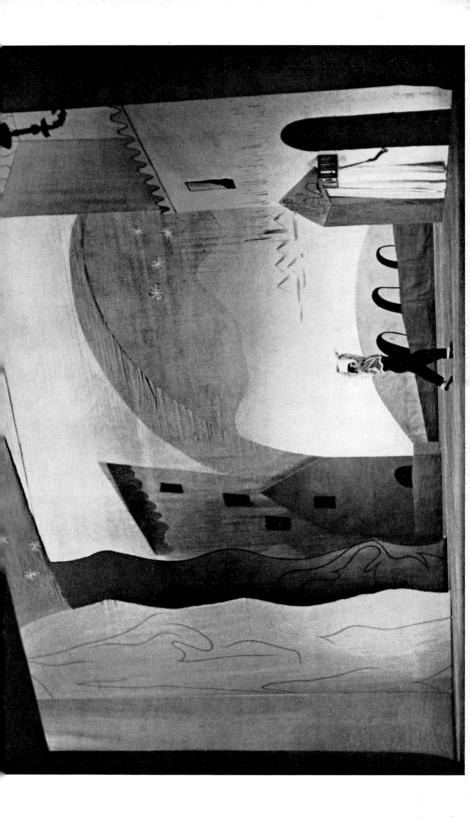

simply as bad and eccentric dancing. To anyone brought up on Ballet, it is a beautiful extension of Ballet Style into alien forms. *Les Matelots* is the commentary of a rather blasé modern mind on Classical Ballet. *Le Tricorne* is rather the commentary of Classical Ballet on its finest purely national counterpart, the Spanish Dance. And so on. . . . Most of the ballets of the Diaghilev Era could be interpreted in similar ways. But I am supposed to be writing a concluding chapter, not starting a new book. Besides, Massine may prove to have only just come to the beginning of his real work. Perhaps the clarification of what is essential in *Choreartium* may still happen. *Les Cent Baisers,* too, though hasty work and filthily served by its music and aggressively sugar-candy decor, brought back Bronislawa Nijinska to the big stages, and there is no saying what may be the influence of her undeviating Classicism on Massine, now that the two are colleagues. This season's return of the de Basil Company from America may quite well change everything that I have diagnosed, here, in the contemporary situation. I hope it will.

Either way, the situation in the Dance itself—considered, that is, apart from its organisation in satisfying theatrical structures—is as encouraging, in any near-sighted view, at least, as the situation in Choregraphy is depressing. Perhaps the one situation causes the other? The idea of Progress is one we still find disgusting, since the century turned, but some such idea is necessary to account for a good many phenomena, not only the Ballet. Every well-trained young dancer, to-day, can do things that, fifty years ago, no dancer could do: thirty-two fouettés, for instance. In *Cotillon,* in fact (which is probably the most perfect ballet since *Les Sylphides*), Tamara Tou-

Damages

manova does not 32 but close on 132 turns, in an alterna-
tion of fouettés and doubles tours. It is as though, by the
powerful operation of Tradition, new muscular faculties
were added to the naturally stupid human body, as though
Tradition, in the Dance, meant a definite organic evolution. It does appear, at any rate, that the present inability
of choregraphers to employ the new dancing forms adequately were an impotence of Mind to cope with Matter
which has become more swift and subtle than Mind.

Certainly, the fixed types are being destroyed. For one
thing, the male dancer has had time to get used to being
the ballerina's equal, both in technical accomplishment and
in choregraphic importance. The work given to the men,
in pre-Fokine times, usually, was eminently depressing.
And the male dancer suffered, stylistically. He was only a
necessary counterpart. The art of the ballerina was fully
developed. His was not. The dancer Massine marked an
epoch as surely as the choregrapher Massine. As a final
gesture, in the Dance itself, the Classical Tradition cast
up Vaslav Nijinsky, who over-rode all its limitations. But
Nijinsky was something in the way of superhumanity, an
out-of-the-way phenomenon. He could teach very little
to dancers in general. And then Massine came along, with
a personal build and style completely matched to the mood
of the time. He presented, in the Dance, the Chaplin hero,
Charlot, the Little Man, the modern Hamlet, the personal symbol of the War years, the focus of its nostalgias.
And he was more effective than Charlot can be in other
realms. As a dancer, he had a superb deftness and physical

Plate 10. Lichine and the de Basil Corps in *Les Cent Baisers*.
(Nijinska.) *Howard Coster Photograph.*

assurance. To assert his validity, he didn't have to paste the floor with a twenty-stone lamp-post-bending villain. He was Charlot triumphant, in his own right. The type has served its purpose, now, along with the choregraphic media evolved to present the type. The lushly exotic type, presented most clearly by Sergei Lifar, has also served. Massine, the dancer, remains a miracle of zest and precision But it is a pastiche miracle. In its place—and Massine himself (the choregrapher) will acknowledge it, if he is to go on producing important ballets—we are demanding the self-sufficient heroic beauty, rarely softened, of David Lichine and, its complement, the steel irresistibility and sheer animal pride of Jurek Shabelevsky.

Above all, though, the technical and stylistic purity of André Eglevsky, who (still a boy of eighteen) elevates like an impalla, pirouettes like an electric drill, is stronger, stricter, than any de Basil dancer and who yet, on occasion, can make the softness of David Lichine's movements look like the articulation of a muscle-bound policeman, on point-duty. . . . It is, above all, an increased nobility of movement—with Nijinsky, perhaps, as an already remote pattern—that we are demanding, now, in the man dancer. And the established type of 'true ballerina'—Russian to the flicker of an eyelash—is changing, equally. There is all the difference in the world, in style and in what we cannot help but call temperament, still, between Vera Nemtchinova, the truest representative of the older school that we have been privileged to see, recently, and Tamara Toumanova, the one of Col. de Basil's three prodigies to reach something like mature perfection most surely. And the fact that Toumanova is only half Russian (half Armenian) is irrelevant, or nearly so. Alicia Markova is a Londoner, but she is unmistakably a Russian dancer.

Shortly, there will be, at last, an English type of the 'true ballerina', distinguished by a specific kind of brilliance and ease, too, not by what Mr. Stokes calls 'the jaunty shyness and simpering jauntiness of the English temperament, so terrifying. . . .' The difference between the Russian and the English danseuse, hereto, has been the very broad difference that the Russian has always been a dancer who happened to be a woman, whereas her English counterpart, though, hypothetically, of equal technical accomplishment, has still been a woman who happened to be dancing. That has been the trouble with English danseuses, that they have been too feminine, insufficiently stylised. The English temperament, as I have argued elsewhere, resists stylisation altogether, in all fields, in a quite peculiar degree. The achievement of inhumanity has always been strangely difficult, for the Anglo-Saxon habit. But there are signs that this national resistance is being overcome, in Ballet, and there is no reason why there should not be, soon enough, not an English Pavlova, but Pavlova's equal in English terms, if the English schools will assert their integrity and stop whoring after Russian mannerisms. At the moment, so far as I can see, our most valuable English danseuse, after Alicia Markova, is Maude Lloyd, whom the incredible stupidity of London managers has, however, confined, till now, almost exclusively, to the tiny Ballet Club stage. About Margot Fonteyn, the Vic-Wells prodigy, it is still too early to be definite, though she will, I fancy, be a very wonderful dancer, indeed, when she has matured herself out of her amazing predecessor's mannerisms. But Miss Lloyd is an accomplished and definite dancer, already, lacking only increased theatrical scope: clarity itself, in line, and with, at the same time, the utmost subtlety and refinement in the qualities of movement. I know of no more perfect piece of work, in the contemporary Theatre, than her dancing in *Jardin aux Lilas*. Alicia Markova is inhuman, with a cosmopolitan inhumanity. She is like the tones of a flute. Maude Lloyd is natively inhuman. Though she bears a Welsh name and comes, in actual fact, from South Africa, she has the clarity of a Norfolk sky.

But then, by our polite cosmopolitans, anything native is felt to be vaguely unnecessary, if not positively trouble-some. The first article of faith, with English balletomaniacs, is that English Ballet is no good, and never will be, because the English temperament, etc. And this childish anti-patriotic snobisme is not denounced, but is fostered, by such minds, well-informed rather than critical, as are responsible for what general rudimentary Ballet Criticism we have. The root, though, of these pestilential attitudes is that this country's zest for Ballet was fired by Diaghilev, while still, that is to say, the Russian ascendancy was un-questioned. And the feeling endures that Ballet not only is now, but always has been, essentially Russian: whereas, in actual fact, like most 'illegitimate' theatre, Ballet (as I was at pains to show, in Chapter II) is Italian by birth, French by upbringing, and Russian only by late adoption. And the further popular doctrine that, in going to Russia, Ballet found, at last, the Ideal Temperament. . . . Surely, this means no more than that the Russian Temperament was ideal for one historical phase of Ballet's growth? In any case, the émigré will soon be absorbed. In any case, the Russian Temperament seems to be turning less Russian, in Russia. And, in any case, since Taglioni and Camargo knew nothing of samovars, there is no ground to suppose that the Future's great dancers will be produced under a five-year plan.

Now that Ballet has scattered, again, the most essential thing to be cultivated, outside pure technical consummation, is regional and national integrity. We must heartily reject Mr. Stokes's statement that 'we want ballet still to be Russian ballet'. We don't, fundamentally. What we want is that Ballet shall still be good Ballet and as rich as possible. And it is only by accepting the limitations and affirming the potentialities of its natural genius that any country can enrich the total medium. All art, at all times, needs roots, needs even nourishment and continuous growth. And it is necessary, for the health of the Dance, as one whole, that we, in England, concern ourselves more with English Ballet than with Russian Ballet. I am not concealing any wish to institute a series of pogroms against the Russians. I say this, not out of any access of Nationalism, but out of the most liberal Internationalism. There is no powerful international idea that does not take its force from the sharpnesses of distinction, within it (like the systems of tensions I have analysed in Ballet itself), of national connotations. As a matter of fact, Russian Ballet, at this moment, is reclining on the glories of its past. As a living and active phenomenon, English Ballet, even now, is more interesting than Russian Ballet. We send off our promising pupils to Paris or Monte Carlo. We are all too ready to applaud and imitate whatever the Russians choose to give us. And English Ballet can find neither the international financial backing nor the impressive cosmopolitan personnel that Russian Ballet can. But English Ballet, even then, is more intensely alive, as a single entity, if only its audiences would acknowledge the fact and not prosecute a complete dissipation of energies. Even choregraphically, though we have not yet produced a cohesive body of work equal to the Russian achievement, there is more cause for patriotic than for anti-patriotic gratification. Russian Ballet —we ought to call it, now, Cosmopolitan Ballet—has only Massine and Nijinksa, at present, and (great names as they both are) neither of them has produced us a masterwork at all recently. Against them, here, we can set three chore-graphers of considerable and greatly varied importance, and they lack nothing, together, but increased scope, increased community with their audiences.

Ninette de Valois, for a beginning, with the Vic-Wells Ballet, has given us three works of quite definitely major importance. In the first place, *Job* and *La Création du Monde*. . . . Not, be it said, that either of these is really Ballet at all. In *La Création du Monde,* especially, instead of the stylistic sheerness of the West's essential Art of Dance, there is stubborn ritualistic mime: the swaying withheld energies of Eastern dancing, without the elaborate system of control of the East's immemorial religious symbolism. And, in an unkind moment, one might offer the supreme reproach that it is a whole-hearted concession to the Central European and flannel-footed. But this kind of thing (though we had and rejected *Le Sacre du Printemps*) has to be done, sometime. We have to get the Negro out of our system and assimilate Hindu gesture and Sir James Frazer, and a painful process it will continue to be, for a while. *La Création du Monde* is dark gods at their best. Miss de Valois controls her difficult material with a force and severity hardly expected from a feminine talent, so that all this purely physiological impingement, this appeal to the solar plexus as the highest tribune, is delicately held, sustained, cumulative, never convulsive. And Milhaud's music, too, is Symphonic Jazz at its best: a polytonal blues that has little in common with the common hysterical nostalgias and the pure sensationalism of—well, of Darius Milhaud himself, when not at his best.

La Création du Monde is dramatically simple, and its problems are choregraphic, only. Such Drama as inheres in Ritual is metaphysical (or ethnological, possibly). *Job,* on the other hand, is dramatically complex in a peculiar degree, and Miss de Valois's own preference for *La Création du Monde* probably derives from a perception that much of *Job's* complexity is adventitious and not germane to her own conception. For—as though the personality of William Blake, who provides a plastic basis, were not already a glass capable of powerful enough distortion—the scenario, by Geoffrey Keynes, has wanton idiosyncrasies of its own. God, for instance, is made out to be Job's Spiritual Self, which is certainly not Old Testament, and hardly Blake, though it may be very good Adler. And this eccentric theology not only provides for spurious dramatic tensions, but also complicates, unnecessarily, the choregraphic problem. Miss de Valois had not only to work up a sustained flow of dancing movements through a series of Blake configurations, but also to establish, within this flow, an objective dramatic for an alien and largely antagonistic conception. Job and his Spiritual Self have no objective relation to each other and so become mere presences, holding dignified postures, which are scarcely developed at all, while the action proceeds round about them (really, inside their heads). The main stress of interest shifts, thus, on to Satan —representing what, in the de Valois-Keynes theology?—

who cannot sustain it in his own dramatic right and so has to have his dramatic importance heightened by every kind of irrelevant means. The figures of War, Famine and Pestilence, having no objective relevance at all (for the theological conception is solipsistic), are completely undramatic, playing an interlude, only.

And so on. . . . The result is that *Job* ceases to be profoundly moving or even coherent Drama—let alone High Tragedy, or whatever name the professors give to the fable—and subsists purely as a major but confounded work of Choregraphy, with pleasant music by Dr. Vaughan Williams and settings, votively prepared from Blake's Illustrations by Gwendolen Raverat, which are only hurt by the costumes (as much a question of material, this, as of colour) of Job's daughters, who thereby become too interesting, plastically, in relation to the sombre masses. This most ambitious of all English ballets, therefore, must be looked on, in the first place, as a magnificent lesson in the misuse, in Ballet, of Literature, judged even by literary standards. Yet there are passages where the dramatic and choregraphic tensions are so powerfully equal as to seem a single absolute: in the episode of the Three Comforters, the episode of Elihu. And this—the definition of one possible kind, perhaps, of essentially choregraphic beauty—is found very rarely, outside Fokine.

And *The Rake's Progress,* a later work than these two, is, apart from its own unique excellences, the first ballet to exploit the many aspects of the English temperament to the full. It is the first true English ballet. Miss de Valois had animated well-known pictures before, not only in *Job* but in slighter ballets, like *Bar aux Folies-Bergère.* And she had done it well. But she had used her pictures as a stimulus

only, and, as it were, a set of props. She had not illumin-
ated either medium. She had not set her two media in any
conscious contrast. *The Rake's Progress,* as well as being a
fine ballet, is a fine piece of Art Criticism. Though as wry
and lively as any piece of dancing, outside the best Massine,
that I have seen, it stresses and stresses again the essential
qualities of pictures. It points to their arrested and frozen
rudimentariness and brings out, into high relief, the peculiar flatness, which no perspective can defeat and which
makes painting, when all is said and done about empthetic
appreciation, an incomplete, a decorative art. The power
to manipulate these qualities in what remains, just the same,
a supremely lively flow of dancing forms suggests that
Miss de Valois has only now begun her work, now that she
has stopped dancing herself, and that a talent of an even
richer and more original kind is beginning to work itself
out. Meanwhile, *The Rake's Progress* has one or two bad
entries, lessening its pungency, and I still wish Miss de
Valois could believe that choregraphic are more important
than dramatic values, in Ballet. But the Betrayed Girl must
be one of the most satisfying parts that Markova has had
done for her, despite the very weak entry in the Mad-
House scene. The whole thing has all the Hogarthian gusto,
with enough reality to tickle the lachrymatory glands into
the proper, the not-too-harrowing Hogarthian activity.
And the opening of the gambling scene, with its deft use of
chairs and its complete translation into choregraphic forms
of the substance as well as the mannerisms of Impatience, is
one of the finest pieces of choregraphy based on everyday
human movements that can be seen. It is better, even, than
the cognate episode in *Les Matelots,* which is very high
praise.

New Perspectives

Frederick Ashton is a talent of a quite different order. It is an order with which I, personally, find myself incapable of very close sympathy. This is no great hardship for Mr. Ashton, since he has come, very quickly, to be accepted as our leading English choregrapher, and I state the fact, mainly, because I believe, from the testimony of some whose opinions I value, that there may be virtues in Mr. Ashton's work that I have missed and that I may, therefore, be guilty, implicitly, of some critical injustice. At any rate, my general criticism of Mr. Ashton would not be in terms of the 'insincerity' that is sometimes diagnosed in his work. It would be, rather, of a certain lack of energy, a certain interior apathy. It seems to me that Mr. Ashton is too easily satisfied. He feels no compulsion to project his conceptions utterly into terms of movement. He is content, very often, with a purely visual presentation. And this, I believe, has sometimes won him greater applause than there was ground for, since, as I have already suggested, an insufficient visual appreciation comes easier to most audiences than the more complex kinds of response which essentially belong to the Dance. That Mr. Ashton's work is important, however, is not to be doubted. At his best, he is almost as good as Bronislawa Nijinska, with whom he has obvious affinities. The supreme sophistication and high polish of his work is always coolly satisfying. In *Les Masques,* he has produced a quite flawless ballet. In *Le Baiser de la Fée,* his most ambitious work, he has produced one episode, the pas de deux in the third scene, which is certainly the loveliest piece of unmixed Classicism in English Ballet or, for that matter, in a good many years of any Ballet. Mr. Ashton is honest enough—and it is a very high virtue—to accept his limitations and neither to strain at more than he can encompass nor to play for loud and obvious theatrical effects. And, above all, everything he does is eminently grateful to dance. It fits the classically trained dancer's body as a Bellini aria fits the vocal apparatus of the classically trained singer.

But the most significant work in contemporary English Ballet may well be neither Miss de Valois's nor Mr. Ashton's. It is necessary, I think, at the moment, to watch most carefully the work that is being done by a younger choreographer, Antony Tudor. Mr. Tudor is by way of being a new talent. His total output is only a half-dozen of full ballets, together with various choreographic interludes for operas and plays. And he has not yet (such is the far-sightedness of the commercial theatre) had the chance to work freely on a big stage. But his work, as a whole, seems to me richer and more pregnant than any other work at present being done, in Ballet; and *The Descent of Hebe,* produced at the Mercury, last season, and not yet offered to the Press (it is felt that it will not realise itself, fully, till it reaches a

---

Plate 11. *The Descent of Hebe.* Hugh Laing and Elisabeth Schooling. The production of such cinematographic effects as this, on the tiny stage of the Mercury, is a triumph of collaboration between choregraphic and scenic artists. Nadia Benois's three ranks of rose-muslin clouds are pulled upward, coincidentally with the falling movement of one dancer, the straining back of another, and an immediate black-out of the stage. The illusion which Mr. Tudor has attempted, with these very elementary means, is theatrically (not naturalistically) complete. Music by Ernst Bloch. *Malcolm Dunbar Photograph.*

larger stage), is, I am convinced the most vigorous piece of choregraphy that London has seen since Balanchine's *Cotillon*. It is Mr. Tudor's distinction to have come to the understanding that what cannot be translated wholly into terms of movement is valueless in Ballet ('translated into' and not 'expressed by'). He uses narrative and poetic literary bases. He has not yet produced the completely abstract ballets that I want to see him produce. But it is choregraphic form—the rhythmically conveyed and nervously intricate impact of physical movement—that matters to him, throughout, not literary expression and not visual titillation. He has shown a great fondness for Greek legend, in all his work. *Atalanta, Lysistrata, Planets* and *The Descent of Hebe* all have Greek sources. But, though the dramatic or symbolistic material is presented with the utmost theatrical sureness, the focus of Mr. Tudor's concern has been, throughout, a stylistic focus, in those precise aspects of Greek movement which escaped such romantic ponderers on the urns as Raymond Duncan.

His highest achievement, so far, is the Fugue which concludes *The Descent of Hebe*. This, isolated from the rest of the ballet, is purely abstract and not, therefore, susceptible of verbal analysis. But it is possible to point to the incredible richness of new movement, of entirely new forms, in it, which are all, none the less, perfectly assimilated. In this intricate Fugue, it seems to me, Mr. Tudor has presented all that is accessible of non-Dionysiac Hellenism, in terms of the Dance, and has yet so perfectly digested it that he is still working within the pure Classical Tradition of Ballet, simply extending its stylistic implications.

The most obvious general stylistic achievement, in what

Damages

Mr. Tudor has so far produced, has been to give the upper part of the body more significance, a wider and more complex range of plastic importance, than it has previously had. The comparative insignificance—more exactly, the purely negative significance—of the arms and torso in Classical Ballet is, in a quite definite sense, natural. It sets the Dancer in a natural relationship with his immediate environment, his (as it were) magnetic field. That which has traffic with the solid ground must be tense, assured, even violent, in its action. That which has traffic with the infinitely yielding air must be infinitely delicate and infinitely unobtrusive. And this is the fundamental pattern of Classical Ballet. In any form of the Dance, in fact, whose most powerful urge is outward, to be wholly objectified, the upper part of the body never can have the scope that the lower part has (unless, of course, we take to dancing on our heads). Otherwise, the muscular tensions, in Space, are disproportionate. This is clear enough, I fancy, if you try to imagine a technique, for the arms, as exacting and as rigorous as the classical technique is for the legs. It could only be an expressive, a mimetic technique. In purely physical terms—that is, in its own terms—it is inconceivable. It might even be proposed, generally (and almost, for the West, as an exact and scientifically applicable standard), that, the more essentially lacking in vitality a form of the Dance is, the more, in its characteristic forms, will the upper part of the body tend, in relation to the lower, to be asserted, to be made to take the main plastic stresses. At the same time, there is every reason why all the implications of the classical technique should be more fully and more variously worked out in the arms and head and torso. And this, in a general way, is what Mr. Tudor has been valuably up to, both in *The Descent of Hebe* and elsewhere.

In *Planets,* the achievement has not been so sharp. The first and third movements, with their altogether convincing and illimitably suggestive presentation of the rarefied physicality of the inter-stellar spaces, are excellent, but their intention is an intention which does not carry forward. The characteristic forms, here, have no implication (as forms) beyond themselves. And the second movement ('Mars'), though projected, as fully as anywhere else, into outward and visible forms, is the correlate of nothing but convulsive sadistic phantasy, coiling back into itself, shuddering out recoiling, eternally inward. But then it is, perhaps, high praise, to say that this movement is the most obscene thing I have ever seen in a theatre. Certainly, it is a quite definite achievement. It is also, for that matter, good pacifist propaganda, though I am sure it was never intended so.

And what actual flaws—flaws of achievement—there may be in Mr. Tudor's work are to be attributed, wholly, I think, to the theatrical conditions under which he has to work. Because he is too much in earnest to do the kinds of pseudo-Choregraphy that the loud and funny theatres want, he is confined, most of the time, to the microscopic stage of the Mercury. This must not be thought to imply any criticism, whatever, of the Mercury. The intense life with which Mme. Rambert makes the work, there, live is one of the major artistic miracles of the age. That small scope has let Mr. Tudor work without hindrance, so far as detail goes. And the later, the more delicate *Jardin aux Lilas* could only have been conceived and achieved in this intimate environment. But it has impeded the broader choreographic sweeps.

Damages

It might, in fact, be better, for Mr. Tudor, at this stage of his development, if he were forced to be thoroughly vulgar. Massine has been hurt by playing to the gallery. Mr. Tudor is being hurt by having no gallery to play to. A certain boldness is lacking, here and there, a certain large-scale clarity. There is sometimes a too fine and intimate presentation of detail.

This dangerous tendency shows clearest in the use—the very sincere and very clever use—of Eastern movements. *Atalanta* was compounded, throughout, of Greek and Asiatic. There are Japanese movements in *Planets* ('Neptune'). 'Night' in *The Descent of Hebe* is very much 'turned-in'. And the fact of working in a little theatre, in intimate atmospheres, has over-subtilised these usages. It has caused Mr. Tudor to work as though Choregraphy were as delicate and as intimate, in its operation, as Poetry: as though these 'culture-references' could be hinted, in a ballet, even more subtly than they are, say, in the verse of T. S. Eliot and Ezra Pound. And they can't. Until the spectator becomes so familiar with the work that he is able to isolate and minutely examine particular effects, he may be conscious of no more than an atmospheric, an impressionistic Orientalism, a general movement inward. The operation is too subtle, the effect too general. If the work had been done in a big theatre, for a big and varied audience, Mr. Tudor would have been forced to make his effects more obvious. The contrasts, the juxtapositions of forms from

---

Plate 12. *Jardin aux Lilas.* (Chausson—Hugh Stevenson— Tudor.) *Left to right:* Antony Tudor, Maude Lloyd, Hugh Laing, Tamara Svetlova, Elisabeth Schooling. *Malcolm Dunbar Photograph.*

different cultures, would have been heightened. There would have been a great increase in clarity. There would, in fact, have been more true Ballet. For Ballet Intime is, after all, a contradiction in terms.

But this is, I say, a circumstantial tendency, only, in Mr. Tudor. Nor is it so marked, in any case, as I may have made it seem. The Fugue, in *The Descent of Hebe*, is essentially big-theatre work, as sharp and altogether outward and cleanly delineated as any choregraphy ever was. I am anxious, in fact, to demonstrate my awareness of Mr. Tudor's potential weaknesses, in case my praise of him—when he has not yet had his due of general praise—should seem at all extravagant or temperamental. For I am altogether convinced that here is a choregraphic talent of the very highest order: potentially, the most important mind in contemporary Ballet. Mr. Tudor is after something—still not clearly defined, perhaps—that nobody else has suspected, yet. He has it in him, I believe, to produce ballets finer than those Massine has given us. He has it in him to make English Ballet, choregraphically, as fruitful as Russian Ballet has ever been and to effect, thereby, a corresponding enrichment of Ballet as a whole. If he is given enough scope, the next epoch in Ballet, as a whole, could be marked, I think, by him. And that's where the commercial theatre comes in.

Or not, as the case may be. . . . That, at any rate, is enough by way of immediate hopefulness. Ballet remains in a state of amazing confusion. The burden of that confusion rests, ultimately, on the audiences. And the ultimate source of confusion, in the minds of the audiences, is the fact that they demand too much of Ballet, that they enjoy it too comprehensively. They demand a comprehensive Fairyland, in which, night after night, they can go and lose themselves and forget the troublesome world of Reality. They need a Ballet which shall provide them with a complete image of Reality, a complete escape from it. Ballet has to provide them with all the delights and all the psychological comforts. It has to fulfil the functions of all the arts and to be a phantasy-substitute for all the vital activities. What, then, can dancers and choreographers do? They are helpless without their audiences. If their audiences demand a comprehensive Fairyland, then they have to provide a comprehensive Fairyland. And we must make no mistake, here. It isn't the ballets like *Le Lac des Cygnes* and *Les Sylphides* that are most comprehensively efficient, as a Fairyland. It's the more 'realistic' ballets, those which provide the image of a recognisable reality, the 'simplification of current life into something rich and strange', and those which depend most richly on their musical, pictorial and literary elements.

How to come out of the state of confusion? That I won't pretend to prescribe. It is certain that the health of Ballet depends, finally, on the health of Society, as a whole. You can't have a completely healthy art in an unhealthy community. The confusion of Ballet cannot be finally adjusted without the adjustment of a more comprehensive confusion. Yet minor adjustments are possible. Greater community between the Stage and the Auditorium is not impossible. And this there must be. Pending the millenium, Ballet will probably continue to be a minority art, but we can see to it, at least, that it is a good and a vigorous minority art. And this depends, more than on anything else, on what it can take from its audiences. Audiences must be capable of giving out energies, as well as receiving impressions. In the traffic of the Theatre, there must be, between the Stage and the Auditorium, the same kind of system of tensions as there is in all the presentational substance of the Theatre. And a right and productive system of tensions derives, most directly, from right response. But right response does not mean increased enthusiasm. It means, on the contrary, diminished enthusiasm. It means, for instance, discrimination. It also means that audiences must not be enjoying too much, all at once. They must thin out their enjoyments. An audience must have had its literary, its pictorial, its dramatic, its purely musical and, above all, its human enjoyments, beforehand. It must have read books, visited galleries, gone to plays and concerts and, above all, enjoyed satisfying relationships with other people, before it comes to the Choregraphic Theatre.

It needs, in fact, to examine the validity of the satisfactions it is getting from Ballet and to eliminate some of them, critically, in order that its enjoyment of the Dance, itself, may be sharper, fuller, more immediate, more essential and—most probably—less frequent. And that—reverting—is where Ballet Criticism comes in. It is where this book, for instance, comes in. For, certainly, it could claim very little other justification. Nobody wants to erect elaborate critical structures, for their own sake. Certainly, I don't. I find it a fairly satisfying activity, but, among a great many other things, I'd much rather be getting on with creative work of my own or assimilating somebody else's. And, in its own nature, the Dance does not need Criticism. It is a simple extension of rich and greedy life, greedy for more life. And its enjoyment, at bottom, is simply the joy in an act perfectly performed. It is Gerard Hopkins, Jesuit, confronted with the kestrel, the windhover, futtore di vento, and

Damages

'—the achieve of, the mastery of the thing!

*Brute beauty and valour and act, oh, air, pride, plume, here
Buckle! AND the fire that breaks from thee then, a billion
Times told lovelier, more dangerous, O my chevalier!'*

It is this, and only this, essentially (infinitely profound, in
itself, with an infinitely non-verbal profundity), and does
not need cluttering round with critical argument. Critical
argument is not the kind of telling that makes it a billion
times lovelier, told. It has to be told in its own terms, in
choregraphic exposition. But the Dance, now, is cluttered
round with so many things so much more obstructive than
critical argument that critical argument becomes necessary
to it. Criticism shackles a free act. When an act is already
shackled, Criticism can be an acid on the shackles.

And certainly there is a peculiar need, to-day, for free
acts. I have remarked, already, on the over-intellectual,
over-critical habit of the contemporary world, and it is to
this that the Dance is specially relevant. We are dominated
to-day by abstractions. This may seem a doubtful affliction.
For an abstraction is normally a useful thing, merely, a
convenient and economical generalisation of concrete experience, as the ideal Circle is a generalisation, able to be
greatly useful in practice, of what is common to all the
more or less circular things in nature. And all words, for
instance, are abstractions, in that they all mean a range of
objects with only the verbally covered aspect in common.
But an abstraction is easily divorced from practical usefulness, as a word may be emptied of sense, and then it becomes a particularly evil kind of fetiche. It withdraws the
mind from fresh and vital commerce with concrete phenomena, induces a deadness in the face of all but intellec-

228

tual reality, closes up the self from new experience. And what makes the mind withdraw itself in this way is, surely, some fear of life? Primitive races, whose lives seem to be one continual sweat of fear, commonly believe that a name gives magical power over the soul of the object named, the Nomen over the Numen. And it is surely a survival of this fetichistic belief which lets the sophisticated modern mind think to defeat the bewildering phenomenal world with a comprehensive abstract?

It is in some such terms, at any rate, that the present strangeness of our intellectual and spiritual life must be understood. The Intelligentsia, to-day, has lost its function in the community, and intellectuals exist, precariously enough, in a world of their own. In effect, they are all convicted, already, of Kulturbolschewismus and shut in a concentration camp. And their activities, there, when not altogether private, take all their justification from critical abstracts. When the painter, for instance, is not festooning across a canvas his own internal organs, the whole bewildered basis of his work is the purest form of abstraction, the geometric. He uses the label, explicitly, Abstract Art. Poets, also, write either in private languages, now, or according to some forestated abstract basis in Æsthetics, so that Poetry is no longer a Criticism of Life, but a Criticism of Poetry. And most of the new music is not so much a created body of work as its own atonal text-book of harmony and orchestration. The critical faculties are dominant, in fact, even in what is called creative work, because the creative faculties are inhibited, by fear or distrust of their own workings. The artist dares to affirm his own experience only when it has been checked by reference to an abstract critical system. We do not enjoy our paintings, poems and musical compositions, to-day, but merely appraise them. We have no taste, in that word's solid sense. We eat with a coated tongue and think out what the taste should be.

And the sub-educated, the middle classes, behave very much like the Intelligentsia. They will not come to grips with that reality, even, which is themselves. Instead, they learn up one or another of the psychologies (more often than not the Adlerian, which is safe), and these are just systems of self-abstraction, which is to say, apparatuses for describing the personalities, behaviour, wishes and discomforts of the self and all other selves in general lowest-common-denominator terms.

But even the great masses, from whom the strength of cultures has formerly renewed itself. . . . They once lived full and vigorous lives, with a traditional regional wisdom whose solidity, whose direct relation with substantial reality, is shown in the vivid concreteness of the language. And now, torn away from those roots, to be organised and centralised in Industry, they cling to the standard intellectual and spiritual article as fearfully as they do to their jobs, to their jerry-built homes, synthetic food and clothes and all the mass-produced soulless objects which are what they can afford. Where they once lived by their own concrete experience, they now debate in terms of the ready-made abstractions tirelessly disseminated by the news syndicates, the B.B.C. and the advertisement campaigners. Or the more enlightened among them perhaps think of themselves as specimens of that sublimest abstract of all, the Economic Man.

Centralisation, Standardisation, Rationalisation, on the purely material plane, however, have been engaged, for a century and a half, in making a single abstract, a comprehensive formula, of the whole physical environment. My statement itself is Abstraction. And This Age or the World in Our Time may well have more important characteristics, in its economic and political structure. But this domination by abstractions can hardly be called unimportant. And it is in relation to this that the Dancer seems to me, to-day, to be a particularly relevant figure. Indeed, it seems to me that Ballet represents, ideally (in its own ideal form) and symbolically, a state, a condition of being, contrasted with the general condition of the World in Our Time in a strangely complete and precise fashion. This, I fancy, is why so many are turning to the Dance, now. It represents (ideally and symbolically) a state towards which all our most valuable impulses can be and are already directed.

For all dancing is urgent and substantial life. Ballet, in particular, is altogether swift and vivid, flaunting, vigorous, eager. And any such condition is the strongest denial both of abstraction and of any loose noisy assertion (such as, to-day, we are equally plagued with). On the one hand, there is virtuosity, but there is no place for the Bigger and Better, the Louder and Funnier, in the art of the good dancer. His patience, his discipline, his energy and his precision are not equalled in any other work of man. And closed abstraction, glib generalisation of experience, apart from practice, is wholly impossible in Ballet. Though a highly developed form of art, and although it works with ideal patterns, the main stress of Ballet is always on the concrete and particular, the full life of the pure phenomenon and its infinite possibilities in sharp and untroubled significance. It affirms, we can say, this truth of William Blake's, that

Damages

'Art and Science cannot exist but in minutely organised Particulars,
And not in generalising Demonstrations of the Rational Power:
The Infinite alone resides in Definite and Determinate Identity.'

Its concernment, above all, is with the disciplined subtlety
and loveliness of the individual human body; and this in an
age whose only common carnal awareness, is either an
hysterically heady and finally abstract exhibitionism and
post-adolescent curiosity, or that furtive self-shame which
is Puritanism's last bequest and by the insidious aggravation
of which the advertisers of a certain soap set themselves
out to fatten its manufacturers' profits.

Perhaps our general hope must lie in the movement there
is among the youth of the great social masses towards a
greater or a renewed concreteness of living, with its necessary part in an affirmation of the whole being, the intricate
significance of the body, most, against the hereto-unques-
tioned ascendancy of the mind. Athletics is taken more
seriously, now, than it ever has been, since Periclean
Athens. The more intensive kinds of Athleticism apart, the
whole of the younger generation, to-day, is concerned to
assert the body's grace and discipline in any of a hundred
ways—all strenuous, though many of them hysterical and
many merely silly—from Sunday hiking to sun-baking and
Nudism.

We have D. H. Lawrence, also, with his ridicule of the
Mental Life, his often over-anxious demand for a subtler
and bolder physicality, a greater devotion to the bodily
nature. And we have the demand of the most popular of
our young poets. Stephen Spender, understanding well the
intellectual stalemate in which his own poetic beginnings
were implicated, desires the overthrow of the intellect's
supremacy and its hoarded values.

232

New Perspectives

'*Count rather those fabulous possessions*
which begin with your body and your fiery soul:—
the hairs on your head the muscles extending
in ranges with their lakes across your limbs
Count your eyes as jewels and your valued sex
then count the sun and the innumerable coined light
sparkling on waves and spangled under trees. . . .'

He envisages political revolution as primarily a matter of
new health, new energy, new grace.

'*Oh comrades, step beautifully from the solid wall*
advance to rebuild and sleep with friend on hill
advance to rebel. . . .'

And the conclusion of W. H. Auden's last solid work, still,
sounds oddly like a definition of Ballet:

'*Where Grace may grow outward and be given praise*
Beauty and virtue be vivid there.'

All these are, in some way, expressive of tendencies working yeast-like in the whole mass of Society, expressive,
therefore, of fundamental needs and stopping, perhaps, a
main gap between the Intelligentsia and the other social
layers.

And the wish is basic, there, to make to Life, in the
round, the kinds of response which are necessarily made to
Ballet. We are needing to get the delight which belongs to
the Dancer out of all the processes of living, which should
be detailed and sharp, impinging straight on the nerve,
without the eternal stress of the inhibiting intellect, and
which should yet be delicately organised in ideal patterns.

Bibliographical Note

Books by contemporaries quoted or directly referred to, in the text of this book, are *Time and Western Man* (Wyndham Lewis); *Collected Essays* (T. S. Eliot); *Balletomania* and *Diaghileff* (Arnold L. Haskell); *Point Counterpoint* (Aldous Huxley); *The Story of the Russian School* (Nicolas Legat); *To-night the Ballet* and *Russian Ballets* (Adrian Stokes); *Son of Woman* (J. Middleton Murry); *Speculations* (T. E. Hulme); *My Life* and *The Art of the Dance* (Isadora Duncan); *Lady Chatterley's Lover* and *The Plumed Serpent* (D. H. Lawrence); *The Meaning of Meaning* and *Principles of Literary Criticism* (I. A. Richards); *Music Ho!* (Constant Lambert); *Phases of English Poetry* (Herbert Read); *The Dance of Death* and *The Dog beneath the Skin* (W. H. Auden); *Diaghileff's Second Decade, 1920-1929* (W. A. Propert); *Music and Ballet* (M. D. Calvocoressi); *Borzoi* (Igor Schwezov), and Stephen Spender's *Poems*. Some quotation is also made from *The New English Weekly* (Michael Sayers); *The Adelphi* (J. Middleton Murry); *The Observer, 1835* (on Taglioni), and *Scrutiny*. Most of the historical books and other books not listed here are to be found in Mr. Cyril W. Beaumont's special list. Valerian Svetlov is not normally accessible, to the English reader. André Levinson may usefully be read in bulk.